The
Faces
of
GOD

The Faces of GOD

ESSAYS ON CHURCH AND SOCIETY

ADRIAN HASTINGS

GEOFFREY CHAPMAN LONDON

GEOFFREY CHAPMAN PUBLISHERS
an imprint of Cassell and Collier
Macmillan Publishers Ltd.
35 Red Lion Square, London, WC1R 4SG
and at Sydney, Auckland, Toronto,
Johannesburg
an affiliate of Macmillan Inc. New York

ISBN paperback 0 225 66123 3

Printed in Great Britain by
Northumberland Press Limited
Gateshead

Contents

Contents

Preface

This year, 1975, one full decade has passed since the close of the Second Vatican Council. The Catholic Church and, perhaps, the wider Christian ecumene as well stand in a more uncertain condition than they have known for long. They share the uncertainty of world society and of the West in particular within an age which will surely come to be characterised by the weakness of its institutional leadership in the state as much as in the Church. There are exceptions—a Julius Nyerere here, a Michael Ramsey there—but they are not many, and they may still diminish. The academics too, be they theologian or philosopher or economist, offer less and less assured guidance. There was an understandable over-optimism at the time of the Council—it too was part of the spirit of that age: 'We never had it so good', the age of Pope John and Macmillan and President Kennedy. All the light of a false dawn, the absurd and depressing light of 'The Secular City'. The Catholic Church's highly providential and fruitful renewal was somehow carried along inside a wider historical moment. Then came the inevitable faltering—a faltering in the Church on many sides and a far wider faltering in society. Faltering followed by disillusion and pessimism. We are unlikely to return to the mood of the early 1960s today or for many a day. But pessimism will get us nowhere. New wisdom and new life are bubbling up if one but looks for them, and there are battles to be fought whose issue is beyond the reach of either optimism or pessimism. The essays in this book are written by one well inside the Roman Catholic communion, one struggling still to hold to, and to share with a friend here or there, the 'Faith once given to the saints'. They are published in the hope that they provide something of a unified message for our time, a sense of direction—moral, ecclesiastical, political—which is intrinsically faithful to the highest sense of christian orthodoxy but, precisely because of that fidelity, can be unswervingly, if never uncritically, radical in the fields alike of social problems and ecclesiastical structures.

Adrian Hastings
January 1975.

Acknowledgements

Chapter 1 began life as a sermon preached in St Francis' Chapel, Birmingham University, 4 March 1973. Chapter 2 was first published in *Concilium*, March 1972. Chapters 3, 8 and 12 have appeared in part in the *Tablet*. Chapter 5 was written as a seminar paper for the School of Oriental and African Studies, October 1973. Chapters 6 and 7 were published in *One in Christ*, January 1972 and October 1973. Chapter 9 was written for an international consultation on mixed marriage held in Dublin in September 1974 and subsequently published in *Beyond Tolerance*, Geoffrey Chapman (1975). Chapter 10 was the Ramsden sermon preached before the University of Cambridge in Great St Mary's, 2 June 1974. Chapter 11 draws upon some articles published in the *Clergy Review* at the beginning of 1973 and by Gaba Pastoral Institute, Uganda, a few months before. Chapter 13 appeared in an earlier form, unsigned, in the *Catholic Herald* at Easter 1973. They have all been very considerably rewritten.

I

The Faces of God

'Now we see only puzzling reflections in a mirror, but then we shall see face to face' I Cor. 13:12.

St Paul admits how little we can understand at present and how very perplexing even that little can be; he tells us that a time is coming in all our lives when this will be changed: 'My knowledge now is partial; then it will be whole, like God's knowledge of me.' What a fantastic claim for the future: face to face knowledge of God. The quality and scope in any life depends upon the degree of knowledge each living being has, and as this knowledge we await in hope is and must be wholly unimaginable—so the future human condition must of necessity be so profoundly unpredictable that even its existence or likelihood almost eludes any category or argumentation derived from our contemporary experience.

Our present knowledge is simply different, yet now too we know not nothing of God, be it 'only puzzling reflections in a mirror'. But even reflections include some hint of the reality, and out of them time and time again man claims to have grasped something, to be able to say something, of that which is reflected. Elsewhere Paul remarks: 'His invisible attributes ... have been visible ever since the world began' (Romans 1:20). This paradoxical experience of divinity whereby our race generation after generation was never without such hints, able to sense the divine attributes through the bewildering complexity of the world we know, yet never able to see face to face, has impelled us to make to ourselves 'faces' for God—in wind and lightning, in sun and moon, in wood and stone, in painting, in the phraseology of human vocabulary. Could we have done anything else? But having done so, can we then do anything else but smash those faces, so remote they inevitably are from what they are intended to intimate? Without seeing that to which they point, and despite the service of a sort they have provided, there yet comes a day when we become overwhelmingly conscious of their inadequacy.

So much so that they often seem to be themselves the barrier blocking our approach to the 'divine'.

It is fitting that we recall one such outburst against the images that repel. Twelve years ago we woke up one Sunday morning to read in the *Observer* that 'Our image of God must go'. It is the twelfth anniversary of Bishop Robinson's *Honest to God*, with its powerful protest against puerile faces of God: the old daddy in the sky, up there, out there. He suggested turning 'down there' instead, to 'the ground of our being', 'ultimate reality', or 'being as gracious', calling to his aid the phrases of Tillich. Did it help much? As a prophetic stirring of religious thinking at a particular moment, yes it certainly did; as a clear step forward on the long road of speaking about God, no, probably not.

Few thinking believers really have an 'up there' or an 'out there' conception of God, or are likely to be surprised that astronauts don't come across him in outer space. Nor is 'down there' any intrinsic advance; indeed, if proposed seriously at all, it becomes a step back, not forward, in that it seems to be willing to propose a spatial conception as being actually of some help in the matter. All these phrases are red herrings, the real central issue in regard to our God talk being other and quite simply this: is our basic image of God to be a personal one or an impersonal one, something such as 'being as gracious' or 'ultimate reality'?

Here the Jewish, Christian and Islamic tradition seems to me to be challenged at its most central point. The decisive assertion of that triple tradition is that God is personal and, therefore, intensely ethical. Within that tradition God has chosen, and put up with, an anthropomorphic mask because—we can presume—it is essential to the sort of task which is primary in the purposes for which revelation mediated through the tradition has been granted. Morality of a sort can be related to a non-personal God, but not the intense crusading concern for the ethical which is the most decisive characteristic of the Judaeo-Christian God.

Only a God who is a person can be a god of persons. Some gods are of natural forces, many gods are of places, but Yahweh was a god of persons: 'The God of Abraham'. In this religion places, shrines, temples were essentially secondary and finally irrelevant. He is a god of persons because he acts on persons, cares about persons, and makes them act. 'I am Yahweh and I will bring you out' (Ex. 6:6). If the mysterious word 'Yahweh' has a definable meaning it is something like: 'I who exist dynamically.' I who get things done.

This was the face revealed to the early Israelites: the face they experienced. At first their God was indeed still one among the gods—sufficient for them, but not for all men. For them too this exclusive sufficiency was difficult enough to live with; difficult perhaps to relate all the divine attributes they sensed, the images, the faces of god they were cognisant of, to just one Yahweh. Hence the temptation to polytheism. Polytheism is one response to the factual experience of the multiplicity of divine faces. Many gods with many faces—each saying, manifesting, something rather different. That was the world of ancient religion, as it is to some extent still the world of African and Hindu religion. Multiplicity, yet also always some hidden unity too: hard gods and indifferent gods, benign gods, remote gods, interested down-to-earth gods, gods who ask for blood, gods who push you to kill and burn, gods who teach you to be patient and forgive.

Many faces for many circumstances and many people. To crowd all this into a single god (even if, and when, a subordinate satan was clearly differentiated and allowed some rope) was very hard: monotheism is not easy in a god-inebriated world. Yet there comes a time when it is clear that there can be no alternative, whether in Israel, in Greece, or in Africa. And so, one God but many faces. Some of them, seemingly or really, contradictory.

The history of god is in part one of deciding which masks he can wear, which he cannot. Which faces were all along a great misunderstanding. That surely is our problem with the Old Testament. If god is tied by his very being as purposeful creator, by the whole point of the revelation, to the ethical, then his faces cannot be too much ahead of the ethical standards of the moment. They will rise together. In the meantime we have to put up with some awful faces for God. Take the holy war and the extermination of the vanquished: 'I mean to make the fear of me go in front of thee, bringing destruction upon the whole people' (Ex. 23:27). 'Be my enemy and thy children to the third and fourth generation shall make amends' (Ex. 20:5). Retribution is to be carried on by this god from fathers to their grandchildren; his people, just one wretched little nation among so many others, is to march in, wiping out their enemies, making of them a 'herem', an anathema—just as the king of Moab massacred Israelites in honour of his god, Ashtar-Kemosh. He too made his enemies an 'anathema', imagining that in so doing he was pleasing the deity.

Under the influence of their neighbours and their own inadequate morality, the Israelites imagined that Yahweh could want the same and even wrote down his instructions on the point. That was one of the faces of God. Perhaps indeed he could teach in no other way, man being the evolving being he is, but it does

3

mean that the sanctioned image of god and intertwined ethic of one age, however authentically part of that mixed-up process the 'history of salvation', cannot be normative, although it is suggestive, for another. An evolving man can only be addressed by an evolving god.

But god is beyond man and in each age his surest spokesman is the far-out man, the prophet, the one sensitive enough to hear something of the divine word for himself, and brave enough to be out of step in consequence. God could not rest content with this awful face for him the Israelites had picked up from neighbours such as the Moabites, the god commanding anathema. Yahweh the just, Yahweh the deliverer, Yahweh the compassionate. Here were truer faces, even if the limited horizons of concern of the people themselves made them tend to limit too the horizons of concern of their god—just and merciful for them, oblivious of others. But the territorial and national limitation too is increasingly transcended—in Isaiah, in some of the psalms, and then—decisively—in the new covenant.

The faces of god cannot neatly be categorised as right ones and wrong ones, only more and less inadequate ones. Even the most inadequate may be saying something right, while the least inadequate are still saying too little. They clash, hint in different directions, speak to different people. This is true of every religion, but it is truest of all in the disorderly wealth of biblical and Christian literature. The books of the Old Testament witness not only to the living but unseen god but to the perennial human struggle with the divine: to penetrate through the complexity, the limitations, the ecstasy and the anguish of human experience —at times its sheer horror—to discern a face of god in which we can reliably recognise the unrecognisable. Yet the face chosen speaks often more clearly of the one choosing than of that which should be behind the face.

Cruel people want a cruel god and cruelty has been one of the most decisive characteristics of human society: the sadism and masochism of the human race time after time create a face of god as cruel as itself. Old Testament theology could not be unaffected by the cruel divinities all around and the cruelty of Israelites themselves. We have seen something of that, and yet surely the deepest, most heart rending struggle of the Old Testament was, indeed, to show that such was a false face of God. Yahweh is not merciless but merciful. Some things never formed part of the official religion of Israel—regular human sacrifice above all. Yet people wanted this too, and at one time were near to identifying Yahweh with Baal or Moloch. There was a great 'roaster' in the valley of Ben-Hinnom near Jerusalem where children were sacrificed in fire. But Yahweh was not that sort of a god and the people knew it in their hearts.

How much man wants religious sanction for his most murderous and sadistic tendencies. How popular the cult of Moloch was, prevalent not only in Phoenicia, but across the sea in Carthage. Here too small children were placed in the arms of the great bronze Moloch before slipping into the flames. Judaism and Christianity escaped the practice, but have they always escaped the preconceptions of the cult of Moloch? Did not something of this side of the religion of Carthage pass unnoticed via Augustine and the church of North Africa into the theology and ethics of western christendom? Did it not minister to the obsession, both Calvinist and Catholic, with predestination, with the nightmare of a god who creates beings, predetermining them to the everlasting agony of hell prior to any fault they have committed; with a god who, it was claimed, condemned the great majority of all human beings to hell? Belief in such a god encouraged and justified an equally ruthless and insensitive ethic for man, at times only too clearly sadistic or masochistic—so hard on the poor, on the unmarried mother, the petty thief, the religious deviator; so insensitive in its confining of the religious 'life of perfection' to those segregated from all sexual activity, so twisted in its insistence upon the virtue of self-flagellation. All this and so much more reflects one particular 'face of God'. Was it not an unacceptable face?

It is certainly true and decisively important, that in the biblical and Christian tradition God-talk is continually reflected in applied ethics, in doing and not doing. It is never a detached, academic God-talk. The face of the God that you meet, you must and will respond to in your own behaviour; so that the judgement of another upon that behaviour is the surest way for that other to come or to refuse to come himself to meet with God.

The central theological struggle across centuries of biblical writing is not the struggle between a person and a philosophical first cause but between a jealous, long remembering, exclusive, cruel god and a forgetful, long-suffering, forgiving, all-embracing god; and thence between a human ethic which offers appropriate service to the one and an ethic acceptable to the other. More and more as the Old Testament advances the latter model appears as the only possible God for Israel. Yahweh is not Moloch. Not at all. The biblical god of wrath is revealed with ever less ambiguity as a god made angry with injustice, and this latter in hard existential terms means man's illtreatment of man. Injustice appears

5

ever more clearly synonymous with lovelessness, hardness of heart, while biblical justice is not a hard legal weighing of the scales and searching of contracts but an enduring compassion. The god of wrath is made angry by lack of love; if this be the formal cause of divine wrath, it can only be that God himself is love, that this word be our finally least inadequate human term for divine assertion. In which case the wrath of God does not offer an alternative model to the God who is love but a sort of intermediate technology devised initially to communicate the divinity of love to human blockheads.

Yet ambiguity remained and the central theme of the New Testament (though even there not wholly unobscured by the human need to divinise cruelty) is surely one more supreme effort to get the record straight: Yahweh's overwhelming apology for all previous misunderstanding. Not the god of armies and of vengeance, but the father waiting on the road to welcome back the prodigal son. Not in power but in mercy is he revealed. And if there be so much cruelty in the world, undeniably God's world, so that the cruelty could plausibly be hailed by the cruel as an expression of the face of God, then indeed without more ado let this cruelty be exercised as directly as possible against God himself. His son will be crucified; then surely, God seems to say, no one will think again that crucifixion or any comparable cruelty could express his nature, instead of being the most outrageous denial of it.

At this point the face of the god of love and compassion ceases to be remote. 'Have I been all this time with you, Philip, and you still do not know me? Anyone who has seen me, has seen the Father' (John 14:8). The face of Jesus is the face of God, so that meeting with the God of Jesus we can hardly cry any more 'Let God be God': it would be one step back from the full meaning of the incarnation. Rather must we say 'Don't make a god of god'. Call him Abba instead. Father, almost Daddy. A personal face, a close face, a human face, an undeniably anthropomorphic face, and yet the nearest thing to the face of the unseen God. Subsequent to the Incarnation we cannot discuss the faces of God, as if there were no Incarnation. It is done and cannot be undone. We have seen. *Deus* is now never *Deus solus*. He is our father whose face shines forth in Jesus Christ, calling yet again—as the biblical God has always called—for the works of justice: his signature tune.

The power and the wisdom of God are discovered not in philosophical abstraction but in an innocent man crucified upon a tree, appealing for forgiveness. Crucified and yet alive. That was

6

unmitigated foolishness to the world of the first century. It has been foolishness ever since. Not then 'up there', nor 'out there', nor 'down there', nor now in Jerusalem, nor on this mountain, nor in Rome nor in Lourdes, and yet in all these places, the depths of your spirit, your inner room alone, where two or three are gathered together, between two thieves, on the road that leads to Jericho (that spot where the old Yahweh was thought to have carried out one of the worst of his massacres), in the least of the socially insignificant: here is the face of God.

'Only puzzling reflections in a mirror' Paul tells us at the end of it all, as enigmatic as the three figures in Rublev's Trinity. Is it surprising if we find all our words inadequate, if generation after generation men cry again: down with the images. Our image of God must go. But where should we go? Upstairs, downstairs, to the religious philosophers, the deists, the pantheists, what have you. They are none of them new. They have been here with their 'ground of being', their 'world soul', their 'ultimate reality', their 'first cause', in every century. The central theological battle of the Christian era, which has had to be fought over and over again, has been that between a personal God and some sort of Aristotelian principle. However the god of the philosophers or of pantheists is delineated in word, its face has always to be non-personal—precisely to escape the wounding charge of anthropomorphism. But by asserting such a face one is always and necessarily repudiating the central thrust of biblical revelation and undermining the whole dynamic, this-worldly cutting edge of that revelation: its ethical effectiveness. Every god whose face is non-personal proves to be ethically as dead as a doornail. Bertrand Russell relates in his *Autobiography* how he was once told an amusing story in the Fellows' Garden at Trinity. His informant remarked to him 'This is where George Eliot told F. W. H. Myers that there is no God, and yet we must be good; and Myers decided that there is a God, and yet we need not be good'. Clearly no one in the story, and least of all Russell himself, was anywhere near an idea of the morals-first God the biblical-Christian tradition has, at its heart, always propounded; but this is not surprising as the theologians have forgotten it as well. With 'ultimate reality' and its fellows we do indeed not need to be good—at least not because of any decisive relationship with 'ultimate reality'; we do not need to cry out in anguish with the whole depth of our being against Auschwitz and Belsen, massacre and torture and terrorism, the children left homeless in the gutter, the sheer hardness of the human heart. No, we can turn back to our glass of port.

Son and Father. The God of Abraham. God made man. The festal welcome to the prodigal. The crucified Lord. It is all indeed childish and anthropomorphic; foolishness to the gentiles; continually teasing. We cannot make it otherwise. And it is not, very clearly, intellectually verifiable in any way dry reason can devise. But then no more is any other god-talk, be it as philosophical as you make it. Yet a living face of God is verifiable in the context of this world in another way—in its factual (not theoretical) moral consequences. The face of God in the face of Mother Theresa, the face of Pope John, the face of Maximilian Kolbe. The central line of Jewish and Christian God-talk has proved to be ethical dynamite in generation after generation, so long as it remains free from the temptations of Moloch upon the one side and Aristotle upon the other. It is only within the context of living, of what God language makes you do, that the foolishness becomes wisdom and a reliable face of God is irrefutably revealed. Here and only here does a denial of God become itself ridiculous. In the old words of Jeremiah: 'Did not your father eat and drink and do justice and righteousness? Then it was well with him. He judged the cause of the poor and needy. Then it was well. Is not this to know me? says the Lord.'

2

Should church reform start from the top or from ground level?

In attempting a reply to this question it is useful to begin by considering the recent process of conciliar reform in itself. Many of the major reforms of Vatican II, as is clear from a study of the first drafts, were hardly desired or intended by those planning it at the centre. Yet the Council agreed upon great reforms, some of which are still in process of implementation, and set the stage for others which are now being fought over; what was done could not have been done without the action of central authority and its authorization. This was largely so, of course, because central authority has had a tremendous blocking power, a power of veto, in the Catholic Church: its negative can be far more effective than its positive force. So a decision at the centre to withdraw the veto was necessary for reform, though positively it is far less effective in implementing it.

It is equally true that the reforms of the Council were mostly not previously desired outside the centre by the majority of the hierarchy, nor by a majority of priests, nor even consciously in most places by the laity. They have subsequently been implemented to a very considerable extent, partly because of the weight of authority at the top, but still more because of the contagion of example spreading from one local church to another. Though it would be a great over-simplification to say that post-conciliar reform has been reform from the centre, yet the centre has made it possible, both by the withdrawal of the veto in various areas and by the provision of general norms. The attitude of docility to Rome remains so strong in senior hierarchs and among the people generally that they have quite rapidly carried out measures to which they were temperamentally opposed, had explicitly resisted for many years, and had hardly now been converted to in their hearts: such is still the strength of discipline within the Roman Catholic communion. The speed of reform and change in attitudes has indeed amazed many non-Catholic observers. On a first view, reform by conciliar and papal instruction appears remarkably effective. It is important then to examine the inherent limitations in such reform from the top.

As a matter of fact, the most significant reforms of the Council were approved not because of a previous majority for them nor because of papal backing, but rather because of the effective and convincing dynamism of a minority who had previously seen the need and now at last had a more or less satisfactory forum: this dynamic group, a relatively small number of bishops and their supporting theologians, came principally from a rather limited number of local churches. A widespread sympathy for *aggiornamento*, fostered by Pope John himself, was gradually transformed through the advocacy of a minority into an overwhelming ecclesial consensus. This could only have been done, at least with this sort of rapidity, in a context such as central authority and a general council could provide. In this way the Council operated as a mechanism of release enabling the new vision and dynamism working in some local churches to influence many others rather quickly. The vision had not come from the top, but it needed the top as a channel of effective communication.

The use of the mechanisms of the highest authority to get reform started, and even dialogue for reform, was particularly necessary at the end of the 1950s just because freedom of speech had been for some time so very much restricted within the Church. In the freer and more permissive post-conciliar atmosphere it has certainly been far easier for an ecclesial consensus to develop, as for regional movements of reform to spread effectively, without the same degree of intervention from the top, or even despite such intervention. Vatican II has in fact generated a church atmosphere of freedom, dialogue, consciousness of the local church and of the need for change, which makes possible mechanisms of reform somewhat different from those which, with regard to the Church as a whole, were necessary fifteen years ago to get anything started at all.

The Council itself, moreover, while initially thinking in terms of reform of the Church as a whole, and indeed continuing so to think, was progressively constrained to discard the preconception that a uniform solution could be offered to problems in almost any field. The diversity of situation between local churches and socio-economic areas made the attempt at monolithic reform self-contradictory. Sheer practical necessity enforced the rediscovery of the theology of the local church: the *ecclesia particularis*, the smaller ecclesial unit with its own characteristic needs and the power to respond to them. Such a staggering statement (in the context of the Roman tradition) could even be made as that the Council solemnly declares that the churches of the east, as much as those of the west, fully enjoy the right, and are in duty bound, to rule themselves (*Decree on Eastern Catholic Churches*, a. 5). The churches of the west, one might add, as much as those of the east. Here and here alone did the Council agree to admit the word 'solemnly' so that it can very properly be held that the most serious affirmation the Vatican Council ever made was this one: the local church has a right to be free—it is not to be bullied by Rome or any other central body. However, neither the theological nor the practical implications of such a statement were adequately realized in the atmosphere of the Council, nor have they been subsequently by the post-conciliar curia; much of the frustration of the Church these last years has come about as a result.

It is becoming ever clearer that reform can only be valid and effective when it is a response to the needs and opportunities of a local church; this is true whether it be reform of the *koinonia*, the communion with its structures of fellowship and ministry; whether it be reform of the *kerygma*, the message for today, its theological interpretation and catechesis; whether it be reform of the *diakonia*, the temporal service which finds man in his needs here and now; or whether it be reform of the *leiturgia*, the explicit worship of the believing community.

Within each field and between each field there are questions of priority, of where here and now to direct one's reforming efforts: to concentrate upon liturgy in a racially torn country may be to betray the *diakonia*, to work up an intensity of feeling about racialism in Sweden may be a betrayal of the *kerygma*. Next, there are questions as to the shape of the reform needed, and there are questions of timing. As regards the latter, there is within a movement of reform an ideal moment when men are ready for much, but which, if it is not seized, can quickly pass and obstinately fail to return. Such a moment is often proper to a local situation. This is particularly true in the area of ecumenism and any system of insisting upon a more or less uniform speed of advance at world level will effectively prevent response to it. If the moment is not seized, an essential element of sincerity is lost, the movement becomes flabby and ceases to be quite genuine.

In the field of liturgical reform two strategies have clearly emerged since the council. On one side is the official strategy, the reform of something which one still persists in calling 'the Latin Rite'. This envisages a decisive continuing liturgical unity to be determined in Rome apart from a few marginal details left to local discretion. This goes so far as to require the sending to Rome for approval of texts of liturgical translations into languages which not a single person in Rome is able to read. After several months they are duly returned as authorized. On the other side is the strategy which holds that the maintenance within the liturgical unity of the 'Latin Rite' of countries so vastly disparate as Ceylon, New Zealand, Tanzania, Peru and Norway on the grounds that they all together form 'the western Church' is pastorally undesirable, and theologically a denial of any sense beyond the antiquarian in a recognition of the autonomy of the 'Eastern churches' themselves.

No one should doubt that the adoption of the principles of the vernacular and of integral popular participation have greatly benefited the Church everywhere. Nevertheless, to a very considerable extent, the liturgical reforms of the last few years can be seen as the imposition of a pattern of worship judged suitable for certain milieux in Europe and North America upon the whole world regardless of a real impoverishment in worshipping life that this has entailed for people whose social and cultural attitudes are strongly different from those of the west. Compare the western situation to that of rural Africa. It has been a chief aim of the modern liturgical movement to make liturgy 'relevant' to a society which is characterized as largely urban, industrial, literate and scientifically minded. It has to be made helpful to people who live in large urban complexes, who hardly know the people in the same street, who are in a hurry with trains to catch, and so forth. In most parts of Africa, however, the great majority of people are rural, they are not in such a hurry, they live in small villages, they know all their neighbours, they read little or nothing, they are not scientifically minded.

The new liturgy is becoming more and more cerebral, so many outward signs and picturesque ceremonies have been removed. One even senses in some quarters a certain contempt for ritual in itself. The West may want a cerebral liturgy, though here too aesthetic and mystical needs are sacrificed at one's peril, but Africa and Asia want a sensible liturgy, something with plenty of symbolism, a rich ritual with varied action and repetitive singing. As to length, it is perfectly clear that many of the liturgical reforms are designed to make ceremonies rather brief, to cut duplication. In the rush and hurry of life in the western world this may be desirable, there is so much else to do, attention cannot be held for long. In the country there is not so much else, people may have walked miles to come to church, they have no television to return to, they want a good show not a skimped ceremony, they are good listeners. Again, understanding is necessary wherever one is, but understanding can take different forms. The western stress today is predominantly upon verbal understanding of every word and phrase used: it is the sort of understanding taught in secondary schools. Largely illiterate people do not look for that. What they seek is a global understanding of what the thing is all about. Sensing the symbolism of an action may be far more important and significant than following every phrase the priest uses. The contrasts here go very deep and could be much developed—though it could be true too that the western world in its deeper and truer self is a lot more 'African' in its continuing worshipping needs than the reformers imagine—but they do show how misadvised is the attempt to reform the liturgy in a more or less uniform manner for the whole world.

Localisation is equally necessary for *diakonia*: the service of human society in terms of development and secular liberation. If the vitality of the Church's fellowship and the fruitfulness of its *kerygma* need always to be manifested in the sincerity and effectiveness of its *diakonia*, this has to be done in very different ways in affluent and third-world countries, in lands ruled by Communists and lands ruled by racialists, in lands where a large proportion of the population are Christian and lands where the Church is a tiny minority, in lands where in the past the Church has been closely linked with structures of exploitation and lands where it has not. A blanket concern for 'development' directed, maybe, by a centralized 'Justice and Peace Commission' can be truly disastrous from the viewpoint of a true reform of the Church's relationship to secular needs and structures. Only the local church can finally judge of its own local *diakonia* or indeed how it should participate, as it must do, in a wider *diakonia*. This is well recognized in Pope Paul's letter on the subject to Cardinal Léger, dated 14 May 1971. Yet, here as elsewhere, the local church and local reform cannot be left without the stimulus and even the judgment of the wider communion. Its failure can produce a counter-sign of more than local dimensions. The secular *diakonia* of each local church is today inextricably interwoven with the widest Catholic witness and its reform may need to be triggered off not only at local but at world level.

Ecumenism, the reform of the Church as wrongly divided, is again something which can certainly not be envisaged in merely local terms and yet which will surely only be very partially effective if it is largely controlled from the centre. The needs and possibilities in diverse areas are so profoundly different. This difference relates to a number of vital factors: firstly, there is the contrast between a region where the great majority of people are either nominally Christians or have descended from Christians and a region where all the Christians together may form five, ten or twenty per cent of the population, living amid and witnessing to a vast committed majority of Moslems, Hindus or Buddhists. Secondly, there is the difference created by the numerical balance between Catholics and other Christians. The approach in lands where Catholics form a great majority, and have perhaps a past tradition of oppressing their separated brethren, cannot be the same as that in places where there is a certain balance between communions, or again where Catholics are very few. Thirdly, there is the factor of the character of the chief separated group with which Catholics are here in contact; pre-Chalcedonian Easterners, Greeks, 'High Church' Anglicans, Evangelical Anglicans, Lutherans, Baptists, and so forth. There is a great danger that the Ecumenical Directory and the tendency to play safe in quite different real situations by clinging to its norms in practice provide a way of behaving here and now very inappropriate for a great number of situations. Fourthly, there is the degree of local division and the balance within the non-Catholic Christian community. There has in practice to be an order of priorities in inter-church schemes for greater unity. Where there is a great diversity among Protestants, ecumenical priorities may indicate a certain holding back in regard to Catholic-Protestant relations by churches which react differently in other situations where Protestant disunity is not so apparent or has already been overcome. Fifthly, there is the amount which has already been achieved in a particular country. Some places began very much earlier and are now further on the road than are others. A norm which here and now may appear extremely bold in one area may seem positively retrogressive in another. Such is the complexity of Christian division that the hopes of real reunion get smaller the more they are related to a world-wide achievement rather than to a local one. The theological issue here is very delicate. The re-establishment of full communion, whose horizons are essentially catholic, cannot finally be envisaged in merely local terms, nevertheless much more local freedom is necessary and today there is in fact a continual tension between a Rome directed ecumenism on the one hand and the varied possibilities throughout the world upon the other.

In the field of structural reform it is again clear how vastly the needs of different local churches vary. The almost universal cry of a 'shortage of priestly vocations' (but not in South India) should not blind one to the fact that the existing situation, the coming needs and the ways in which they can possibly be met, are all different. Thus a shortage of vocations means one thing in Holland and quite another in Chile, because the whole background of the Church and existing priest/laity ratios are so different. The structural needs of any one group of churches must not be judged in terms proper to those of another. Thus in most parts of Africa (as of South America) the number of ordinations is and has been pitifully small, but the existence of tens of thousands of married catechists—some of whom have had a training course of two years or more—presents (as in Asia, but not elsewhere) a highly important existing structural element lacking in many other more developed churches.

Any attempt to lay down from the centre a single pattern of structural reform for the whole Church could not possibly succeed. It would not really be practical even within a single area. Take eastern Africa, for example, and three dioceses within it: Ndola, Kigoma and Masaka. Ndola diocese in Zambia includes the copperbelt; it is a relatively wealthy, predominantly urban society with towards a million people, perhaps thirty per cent of whom would claim to be Catholics. It has in all some seven local priests and hardly any seminarians. It has also very few catechists, but many fairly well-educated lay Catholics in well-paid employment. Kigoma in Tanzania is a quickly growing young diocese with over 80,000 Catholics covering an extensive, poor and wholly rural area with some three local priests but many catechists, some rather well trained. Masaka diocese in Uganda is a relatively small, fairly prosperous and densely populated area with some 300,000 Catholics (over half the total population), about a hundred local priests (many of them rather old) and a large number of catechists who have either no training or very little. Listing other dioceses one could continue to ring the changes, though the pattern of Kigoma is more characteristic of Africa as a whole than that of Masaka or Ndola. Sound reform of the ministry must start with the present position, making use of existing resources, not unnecessarily distressing those who are already trying to do the job, and so forth. The needs and opportunities of Ndola, Kigoma and Masaka are obviously strikingly diverse and could not be properly tackled with a single formula, yet all have a very strong need for structural reform of one kind or another.

The guidance of a Roman 'Directory' can often help us little with the true business of effective reform, indeed it is more likely to obscure the real problems and needs of a particular area by identifying the reform proper for a certain ecclesial or cultural area with reform as such and by diverting the limited energies of well-intentioned reformers into tackling what in their own local context are really pseudo-problems.

Yet it remains true in the post-conciliar world that some local hierarchies, clergies and people remain psychologically so Rome-orientated, and so uniformity-orientated, that they may do next to nothing if they are not clearly directed by Rome. Hence, as a matter of fact, it is true that in some areas if there is not reform almost imposed from the centre, there may still be no reform. In the field of ecumenism, for instance, it is still the case in some parts that Rome-inspired efforts have as alternative almost no efforts at all or (perhaps) efforts by a few people effectively vetoed by the authority of the hierarchy. For at the level of the national hierarchy, just as at that of the universal Church, the effective power of higher authority is often one of veto rather than one of positive action.

The Catholic Church is necessarily a subtle balance of local church and universal communion; its continual reform, being an integral element in its healthy life, has to share in this balance. It is most necessary that local churches should be open to the influence of the whole and of the centre, and there are decisions of living as well as of believing which are fittingly taken at a universal level, and so it has always been. Local churches must not be in bondage to the world Church and to the see of unity (though such has for long been nearly the case), but they must not be mentally schismatic either, unwilling to accept a wider consensus, a call for reform or a ruling from the apostolic college or its head. There needs to be a continual give and take, in which initiatives come most frequently from below but the ruling of conflicts and the decisive fiat to change major pieces of existing discipline come from above.

There are indeed decisions which need to be taken at world level, both because of the nature of the Catholic Church and because of the increasingly inter-involved character of modern world society. The very sharing of problems by local churches at the level of the *Catholica* generates a deeper sense of their meaning, greater determination to resolve them, and at the same time builds up the reality of catholic communion. Reform cannot be purely local and a determination to make it so would truly be schismatic. The world Church has to influence local churches, and perhaps trigger off their self-questioning. Equally, local churches must influence each other, from parish to parish, diocese to diocese, and national church to national church. Of its nature, the contagion of reform spreads from one to another, but has continually to be adapted in the process—the unadapted adoption of Dutch reform or American reform in India or the Congo is just as wrong as the adoption of 'Roman' reform. In most things the decisive pastoral judgment has to be a local one, and the final effectiveness of any reform has never depended upon Pope or Council but upon the zeal, contemporary faith, and sense of realistic adaptation of the local ministry and Christian community.

Finally and supremely, reform is super-eminently the work of the Holy Spirit; the renewal in life with which above all we associate him. He is present in all living members of the Church, in those 'above' as in those 'below'. He is above the one, below the other, and breathes where he will. He may grant the charism of a reformer to a Catherine of Siena or to a John XXIII, to a Vincent Lebbe, a Francis of Assisi or a Cardinal Bea. It may be a village catechist one time, an archbishop and chairman of an episcopal conference the next. The charism of the reformer is an almost infinitely varied one and in a Spirit-guided Church we cannot say where it is next to be found. But where the spirit is, there will be the body—the structural shape of a particular reform will depend to no inconsiderable degree on the position within the Church of the one who has this time been given the outstanding charism. One time the vision, the dynamism, the new creation may issue from the lowest of grass roots; another time from the chair of Peter. We can only respect the freedom of the Spirit, but we can be sure too that he will respect our freedom, the dynamics of human society and the diversity of our predicament within the *ecclesia ecclesiarum*.

3

Marginality

Every society has its boundaries and its margins just as it has its central roles and its establishments, and in the end for a society to be understood aright, it has to be considered in the light of both: not only what its main stream and its establishment are doing, but also what is happening to the people in the margin—what they are doing and what is being done to them.

It was a theme in Thomas Merton's later conception of the monastic life that the monk should be a marginal figure, and surely the traditional monastic call to flight from the world, that is to say from normal human society, implied just this: the monk has opted to be a marginal person, outside the regular procedures and categories, someone on the fringe with all the danger and the power that this can bring. Perhaps a basic criticism of the institutional monasticism should be that it has seldom remained faithful for very long to this sense of social non-status: the monk flies to the desert in one generation, but he turns up in the corridors of power, maybe indeed in the House of Lords, in the next.

In the last few years (shall we call them them those of the post *Humanae Vitae* situation, but that of course is an over-simplification), one noticeable process going on in the Catholic Church has been precisely the marginalisation of a new group of priests and lay people whose views on this matter or that seem so out of tune with current official teaching that they are either pushed out of normal positions of influence and ministry or indeed feel obliged to resign from them. Some, it is true, leave the visible communion almost completely but many remain on in the margin, sources of alarm to some, maybe of inspiration to others.

Professor Mary Douglas has provided in her fascinating but often irritating work *Purity and Danger* some analysis of the position of marginal beings in one society and another. They do not fit within a precise category; they are not quite clearly in or out; they are unpredictable, bearers of power but also of possible pollution to the society as a whole. People in such a position may be thought, often rightly, to be upsetting, endangering the society; they need to be guarded against; but they may also be a source of blessing, of new strength and wisdom. She herself relates the margins chiefly to the dangers of pollution, but it seems clear that if some marginal beings pollute, others in fact purify. Marginality may be a danger to the society but it may also be the road in of divinity: the diviner (and the divine) as much as the witch may stand in the margin —not perhaps a Regius Professor of Divinity but at least a Jeremiah.

Such ideas may help us, I think, in an analysis of the Church today. It is true as much as ever that people who seem to some to have drifted to the fringe and to be now merely pollutors, confusing the body, may seem to others guides to a new purity and authenticity. The early friars, marginal men of the thirteenth century, were damned as much as they were welcomed. The prophet who can keep just his foot in the door may let in the light, irritating and out of order as he will surely seem to the hierarchs and the canonists. They would be only too relieved if Hans Küng would do a Charles Davis and get clearly out (though, of course, Charles Davis is not, happily, 'clearly out': he has retained and dug into his own marginal camping-site; whether he was wise to go quite so far as he initially did is another matter).

The marginal ministry is surely a main *locus* for celibacy; here it finds full justification as it does not in the regular pastoral field or in the presidency of the eucharist. It encouragingly allows for marginality, indeed of its nature it asserts it, separating one at once from so many of the normal relationships of society. The celibate can, of course, remain solidly within the system—the system being so devised as indeed to centre around him. There is great danger of unhealthiness in this. If it be a religious system it will almost certainly as a consequence imply an identification of religion at its fullness with the celibate state and go on from there to suggest a certain necessarily imperfect character in the married. Sex will become something quasi-sinful. The proper place for the celibate is not at the centre of a religious system, but at its social periphery: a *memento*, a watch-dog, a profoundly serious hint at the inadequacy of what the system itself is necessarily up to its eyes in. From this point one does not in any way condemn or judge

special power, it is therefore naturally fitting for the manifestation of the mind and power of God to whom all human systems belong except in their corruption but whose freedom and transcendence require continually that we have an outside-the-system-spokesman to prevent the divinisation of the establishment. Such a ministry is lost to the extent to which a rigid rule, the accumulation of corporate wealth, institutionalised links with the rich and powerful elements in society, undermine the effective freedom and social otherness of those who have accepted such a calling.

Many monks and nuns seem almost to have forgotten this deep sense in their calling. They started marginal, but have drifted back into conformity with the world and may even resent the suggestion that this is where they really belong and where, in consequence, they can never be redundant; but others find themselves so placed—some almost willy-nilly—unprotected as the frontiersman always finally is, with all the pain and the opprobrium and perhaps the personal disaster that the state of marginality can bring with it.

Societies and their official leaders rightly tend to be concerned with their boundaries, anxious to maintain the fences and suspicious of those there situated. If they aren't customs officers such people by their very condition almost inevitably provide a blurring of the society's image of itself, a polluting factor, some challenge to the existing certainties which authority both represents and maintains. But in fact societies are not static; their principles of cohesion alter; they grow upon one side and limbs fall off upon another. It is here too that marginal men are so important; if they seem to threaten the present order, they may yet be growing points for a new one. Looking back a century later one sees that some of the people who seemed at any given time to stand upon the margin are found to have been at the very centre, a centre of new growth, while some who at the time are only too clearly at the heart of the institutional establishment have faded into a limbo of unmemorable irrelevance. Père Congar seemed pretty clearly on the margin of the Catholic Church in the early 1950s; only twenty-five years later we can already see how central to a decisive new growth he really was, while the names of his persecutors in the curial establishment are already nearly forgotten.

It is no use becoming too inflamed with righteous indignation about every instance of this sort of thing. The mechanisms of a society require that in any period of stability there be an establishment and that other people be relegated to, or choose, marginality. Some of them really will be bearers of an unwholesome pollution. True marginality is sure to be painful and can be frustrating; those who choose such a condition or have it forced on them can easily feel that they are now seen as a mere cause of internal pollution, to be discarded altogether. Yet if marginality is dangerous it is a needed condition, an area from which comes new inspiration, from which the characteristic onesidedness of this society is exposed. A society which ruthlessly crushes its margins or in which no one freely goes marginal or in which the insight of the margin, its saving unrestricted vision, never gets back to the centre, such a society is in a very unhealthy state.

Such a view of things should encourage those who find themselves, perhaps reluctantly, driven to the margin not to withdraw altogether. Their opportunity to witness to, and work for, the things they hold important is likely actually to grow as they slip into the woods and hills of the border—so long as they do not go right over the border: if they do so they cease to be marginal members of this society and they lose their circle of sympathy, their public, their congregation. Those too at the institutional centre should be helped by a theoretical understanding of the phenomenon of marginality not to be blind to the value of the partial dissident, the anomaly, the man who has moved out from the regular working of the system without sundering all formal links, irritating as he may often be to the hierarch. The wise sheriff will occasionally pay a friendly visit to Robin Hood's camp in the woods. Jesus himself was after all the very type of the marginal figure: unmarried in a society where marriage was a religious duty, the bedless wanderer with nowhere to lay his head, neither priest nor lawyer yet someone who claimed authority beyond both, a prophet from Nazareth, from where prophets did not come—a very anomalous figure, very dangerous but very divine.

4

The predicament of the Catholic Church today

'What!' he exclaimed, 'would you criticise *Propaganda*?' 'Yes,' I replied, 'and greater than *Propaganda*.' (Walter McDonald, *Reminiscences of a Maynooth Professor*, p. 351.)

We stand today within a period of undeniable ecclesiastical depression. Perhaps this demonstrates only too well how much the Church is part of the wider society: our depression is but another side to the fearful questioning and sense of lost direction so characteristic of secular society in the 1970s. For the Roman Catholic Church the movements that brought about the renewal of the second Vatican Council ten years ago and the great figures that led us then are now part of the past. If a few are still happily with us—Suenens and Butler among others—we feel that they have not much more to say to us, and hardly any new leaders have emerged these years in the episcopate, at least at more than local level. Archbishop Helder Camara is surely the one great exception here. The theologians too have aged, tired, faded away. The work of the second Vatican Council was not a failure, though it was characterised by deep ambiguities and considerable inability to challenge some of the most defective of church structures in an even remotely practical way. Yet much was done and probably not much more was possible at the time. Today in the 1970s it is no more possible to go back upon the major decisions of the Vatican Council than it is upon Reformation or Counter Reformation. It is now part of our history, but just because it is so, it already offers us remarkably little immediate guidance on our own problems. Or, if it does, it points two ways. Harping upon its texts can already provide an alternative to an honest facing of the contemporary world. One can bury one's head in the Vatican Council as much as ever one could in the Council of Trent.

Words, words, words, and little more. If that judgement has some applicability to the Council it has far more to those costly and ineffectual efforts that have taken place since the Synods. It would be very hard to point to one single significant decision that has come from the four of them. They would appear to have been cunningly devised as a subtle way of defusing debate and throwing a collegial smokescreen across the unchanging reality of Roman power. For centuries the Catholic communion, the central earthly embodiment of the *Ecclesia* of Christ, has been twisted and corrupted by a consistent policy of governmentalisation, centralisation, Romanisation. In theology and canon law, in liturgy and ecclesiastical administration, in every aspect of the Church's life and practice the Roman juggernaut has gone steadily forward: enforcing uniformity, while admitting by special privilege some trivial exceptions here or there; monopolising the appointment of bishops; substituting the hard discipline of government for sacramental communion as the real nexus of church unity; inculcating the conviction in every loyal Catholic that the only reliable measure of catholicity is the measure of *Romanitas*.

One can see the process at work already in the Gregorian Reform of the eleventh century; one can see it still more in the canonical and curialist developments of the fourteenth and fifteenth centuries against which, indeed, the explosion of the Reformation was in such large part directed; one can see it again in the central thrust of the Counter-Reformation and then in the ultramontane renewal of the nineteenth century. One can see it in Vatican I and very much in the following forty years: the age of Pius X was a high water mark for the Romanisation of the *Catholica*. Much of the movement was unconscious; many of its individual steps can be reasonably defended as a proper response to moral corruption, erastianism or the threat of schism. It is not a history of villains, and its servants included saints as well as some pretty unscrupulous people, but it was a steadily one sided movement which had finally produced by the twentieth century a Catholic Church with a bankrupt ecclesiology which reflected and justified a reduction of the glory of Catholicity to the rigidity of the curial interpretation of the mission of the Church of Rome. Of course this reduction never could be complete. The sheer size of the Catholic Church, the vigour of the old local churches of France, Spain, Germany, Poland and elsewhere, the unloseable presence of the Holy Spirit, all saw to that. Yet each time the tide came further in: Avignon beyond Gregory, Pius V beyond Avignon, Vatican I beyond Trent, Pius X beyond Pius IX, and Pius XII beyond all others.

The Holy Year of 1950, history may well decide, marked the extreme point of the twentieth-century tide—Holy Years always are an occasion for the whipping up of the ultramontane spirit. The proclamation of the Assumption, the world wide devotion to Our Lady of Fatima, the emergence of Catholic Action as a disciplined lay force controlled by the hierarchy of a sort never achieved before, at least since the crusades, the direct appointment even of the Patriarch of the Maronites (a crucial breaking in of Roman control to one of the few areas which had hitherto remained relatively immune), the development of the papal teaching office onto an almost weekly basis: all this characterised the long rule of a man whom we grew up to revere and fittingly revere as a prudent, immensely conscientious and austere father figure, forever at work: A lonely diplomat whose experience was almost purely Roman, whose presuppositions were of an unquestioned ultramontanism, his immediate preoccupations unswervingly anti-communist.

Yet at the same time new things were emerging in different parts of the church: forms of lay apostolate very different from either the sodalities of the past or the official 'Catholic Action' of the present; an immense renewal in the liturgy and in people's attitude to it; a fresh theology, the 'nouvelle théologie' of the fifties—so much under suspicion in Rome at the time—the work of Congar, De Lubac, Rahner and so many others. In the last tired years of Pius XII a fairly considerable effort was made to suppress much of this, but the influence of these men had already gone too far, penetrating even the Secretariat of State and reaching Mgr Montini. The suspect theologians of the 1950s were to become the unquestioned lights of the Vatican Council and the Church of the 1960s.

By 1958 and the death of Pius XII the Catholic Church was frustrated enough, its Roman leadership barrenly suspicious of the best of what was going on—even Montini had been sent away to Milan; but the life was there, bubbling up as it had not been for decades, and Pope John had only to wave his wand, pretty unaware of what the consequences might be but serenely optimistic all the same, and the vast movement of conciliar reform would be under way, incorporating into the official thinking and structures of the Church so much of what was best in the theology and experience of the past fifteen years. A revolution in ecumenism, in liturgy, in ecclesiological doctrine and in much else was the result. Religious freedom, collegiality (a new word for a mild form of ecclesiastical democracy—but let us not forget that democracy's true home is the Christian and Catholic Church), pluralism, the people of God, the word of God—how much was exhilaratingly affirmed or reaffirmed, renewed, discovered almost as for a first time.

The conciliar experience was, of course, very varied and uneven. The Council's documents are a patchwork of new and old —as any such documents must be; they reflect a wide range of theologies and some next to contradictory thinking; they include much very poor writing as well as some magnificent passages. Today they can be appealed to from a variety of conflicting standpoints. Inevitably they started up lines of thought and of ecclesial development which were left incomplete, often hardly more than implicit in some declaration of principle or a timid first step in a line of practical reform. Only in the field of liturgy has there been a really consistent and systematic follow through; much of this has been splendid, yet much of it too has been far too systematic and even insensitive to some of the greatest values of the Catholic worshipping tradition. But this very serious and destructive element of failure in the liturgical reform of the last ten years has been itself largely due to the Roman and curialist way in which that reform has been carried out—even when making use of the latest naive American and Dutch enthusiasts. Elsewhere there has been a very different story with a rapid falling away at the official level in post-conciliar momentum from the end of 1967, though at the grass roots movement has never ceased and a few local hierarchies together with one or two ecumenical bodies (most notably the Anglican/Roman Catholic International Commission) have genuinely continued to press forward.

One striking theme that comes back again and again in the conciliar documents is that of a rediscovered pluralism, the sense of the church being truly a fellowship of diverse churches, a *communio ecclesiarum*. This was very different indeed from the preconciliar orthodoxy of total insertion of all of us in the one *Ecclesia Romana*. It took the Council some time to gain the courage to come to the point of talking about the 'local church' and of 'churches' in the plural, but it did so, and in so doing broke away for the first time in any official Catholic document from the trend of centuries to centralise, latinise and render monoform the Catholic communion. The conciliar stress really was upon catholicity not upon *Romanitas*—a catholicity which can only be meaningful if it goes with an affirmation of ecclesial freedom, corporate as well as individual, of governmental decentralisation, theological pluralism, liturgical and ministerial diversity.

Vatican II sketched the model for a pattern of church life vastly different from that which we had grown up to take for granted and which had tended in practice towards a complete reduction of all public ecclesiastical initiative to the action of the Pope through the Secretariat of State, the working of ecclesiastical administration within and diplomacy without.

Many individual changes agreed upon at Vatican II were compatible with either of these two models—indeed many fit in only too well with the old model which never ruled out prudent change when imposed from above. The conservative diehards were never the true curialists. It used to be said that in the Roman Catholic Church everything is forbidden until it is compulsory; that is no more than a slight caricature of the curial view, which could absorb most of the trappings of Vatican II easily enough. It is disagreeable to see bishops who previously thundered against the use of the vernacular in the liturgy now coming down hard on Latin mass enthusiasts; but it is a typical expression of the old ecclesiology. The one thing it could not tolerate was freedom and diversity. And yet the true message of Vatican II is not one of precise individual changes: it is a reaffirmation of the ecclesial necessity of freedom and diversity.

It was some two years after the ending of the Council that the lines of division again began to become clear and since 1968 we have witnessed an increasingly painful situation wherein the Pope and the Secretariat of State upon which he greatly depends in practice have shown themselves quite unable to absorb the central theological insight of the Vatican Council or to escape from the constricting limitations of the Roman tradition and embrace the vision of a wider catholicity. As a consequence they have destroyed the confidence between the hierarchy and the theologians so wonderfully and fruitfully engendered during the years of the Council. Upon issue after issue they have taken up that position which conformed most closely to papal tradition in the immediately pre-conciliar period in a way which has betrayed far deeper principles of Christian concern and revealed a decisive failure to comprehend both our times and their needs.

Never has the church had to pass more rapidly from a leadership of hope to a leadership of despondency, and that at the hands of a man whose high sense of Christian and pontifical duty no one can question. Surely few popes have had a more difficult age to face than Paul VI and his handling of the Council deserved much praise and gratitude. But trained as he has been through a lifetime of work in the Secretariat of State, surrounded by other men from that same tradition, cut off from effective contact with almost any other circle within the Catholic Church (let alone outside), affected by a fairly advanced age, formed in the school of Pius XII, he has allowed the latter years of his pontificate to become a period of acute ecclesiastical depression to whose true character it would be wrong and irresponsible to close one's eyes. Far too much is at stake for one to have the right further to keep silence before such a tragedy of ecclesiastical decline, irrelevance and futility.

Some years ago, about 1965, I was speaking in Rome with Archbishop Sigismondi, the Secretary of *Propaganda Fide*. I had told him of some disquieting things happening in Africa. 'Why do the bishops never tell us these things?' he asked and then immediately continued, 'I understand, because we do the same ourselves. Only last week I was talking to Dell'Acqua (then *sostituto* at the Secretariat of State) and he told me something very serious. ' "I suppose His Holiness has been told about that," I said to Dell'Acqua and he replied "Oh no, we never tell His Holiness things like that." ' Mgr Benelli is *sostituto* now, and his constricting influence these last years has been grave indeed.

It would be foolish to blame all the troubles of the Church upon the Roman Curia. It is only too clear how much the bishops are responsible—particularly the bishops of Western Europe and the United States; how glad many of them are to have to take no major initiative themselves but to leave as much as possible to Rome; how anxious they are to maintain the ecclesiastical status quo. It is clear too how widely the clergy are to blame, lethargic, suspicious of any threat to their status or financial perks, at times ignoring even the clear decrees of Vatican II. Theologians too are gravely responsible—impractical in their proposals, inadequate in their learning, pompous in their claim to status, greedy for their lecture fees, and impatient when their proposals are not at once implemented. Too many, when they have not quickly been given their way, abandon their ministry and so seem to cast doubt upon the seriousness of their commitment or the importance of their cause. It is clear that the whole Catholic people are responsible if the Church is faltering in its mission, and yet that faltering—it must equally be said—is only partial. The Holy Spirit will not leave this body of Christ and we can see well enough the strength too and the new growth in unexpected places these last years, above all in South America, the Caribbean, parts of Africa and in India. But this new growth which may in the long run be far more significant than the tired rearguard action of the old order owes next to nothing to Rome.

For, when all has been said in blame or praise of other bodies in the Church, it remains a fact that as things now stand it is of the nature of our Catholic system, not so much as it has to be, but as those who have established control over it make it to be, that praise and blame must in particular be related to Rome. In what follows I will consider a number of examples to illustrate our present unhappy condition.

Perhaps the greatest practical failure of the second Vatican Council was in not providing a new method for the appointment of bishops. The traditional and proper Catholic method is, of course, one of direct election by the clergy and/or laity of the diocese concerned, with some possible cooperation from neighbouring dioceses, and this was normative until the very close of the middle ages. The medieval bishop, however, was too often an important political figure whose feudal or civic functions almost overshadowed his ecclesiastical ones, so that his appointment became a matter of major importance to king or emperor. Papal appointment was seen as the only alternative to royal control and in many cases it doubtless was. It could well be justified on occasion but as a system it was being recognised as a serious abuse already in the fourteenth century and it was strongly resisted. In practice the number of bishops appointed by Rome remained small until the late nineteenth century. It was only with the gradual disappearance in the last hundred years of the 'system' of governmental appointments, in fact acquiesced in by Rome, and still surviving in a very attenuated form in Spain and Portugal, and with the vast increase in the number of dioceses throughout the world in the twentieth century that the modern pattern emerged whereby some six bishops are chosen in Rome every week.

Incidentally it is striking how easily Rome did in fact come to accept governmental control of episcopal appointments, so long as this was done in agreement with the papacy: it is clear that this came to be preferred to any system of freedom for the local church to make a choice itself.

One of the central themes of Vatican II was collegiality: the sharing of authority by the 'college' of bishops seen as the successor to the 'college' of apostles—a model very different from the monarchical one, with the Pope at the top and bishops as little more than his delegates, which had been largely taken for granted in previous years. But in practice the concept of a college means little if all the members are appointed by its head. The papal appointment of bishops suited a 'monarchical' ecclesiology; it is quite out of place with a collegial one. Unfortunately the Council, while making great strides at the theoretical level, was extremely weak here, as elsewhere, on *praxis*. Bishops, while truly representing the whole church and apostolic authority in relation to their own dioceses, should equally represent their dioceses, the local churches, in relation to the world church, in episcopal synod and general council. This is simply not credibly the case with the present system, even after the very weak type of consultation which is now meant to take place in a diocese before an appointment.

It is only too clear in practice how careful, and how Roman, episcopal appointments have been during the last ten years. This may not be so noticeable in the more virile ecclesiastical areas of the Southern hemisphere—though some appointments there have been only too questionable—but in the North at least we suffer today from a still more colourless, more docile, more essentially Roman episcopate than we did even ten years ago; and we will continue to do so while the Church at large goes on submitting to the Babylonian bondage which Roman imperialism has inflicted upon almost the whole Catholic communion.

Bishops multiply but priests diminish. In spite of the population explosion, in spite of the continued steady growth in the number of nominal Catholics throughout the world, the total number of priests steadily falls year by year. It did not used to be the case. It has become so only these last ten years—an expression of the deep disillusionment of the clergy with its leadership since the end of the Council. Some of this is inevitable, given the anachronistic character of clerical life and training as it has been for scores of years. It is impossible that an awakening should not bring with it considerable losses. Men who were hurried as small boys into minor seminaries, isolated as far as was possible throughout the whole of their ill-conceived training from almost every secular influence emanating from the contemporary world, taught from the dreariest of second-rate manuals, expected to rely on a self-validating and self-protecting system of Latin mass, stipend and breviary, cassock and celibacy, the respect of the title 'Father', the hearty in-world of clerical companionship, the half day on the golf course, the deanery meeting, the whole self-sufficient society from bishop and remote monsignorial acquaintance at the curia to house-keeper and the Legion of Mary—such men were not surprisingly swept off their feet by so much of what has been sanctioned these last ten years, particularly in the less stuffy corners of the Church. What is rather surprising is how many men have re-adjusted their attitudes and magnificently weathered the storm.

The system as a whole has already cracked wide open, the old men clinging to the remembered routine while they await retire-ment, the young men threshing round desperately for new roles and new meaning. Some do indeed find it in one type of ministry or another, but few indeed are offered really helpful guidance or a sympathetic hand from their bishop when they slip; and in the pressures of modern society, with cassock and collar seldom to be seen, with Christian names everywhere, a deplorable train-ing behind them and next to no leadership ahead, they do slip. At the very least they want support, companionship, someone with whom to share their ideals and the good work they are trying and sincerely want to do. For many that comes to mean marriage, and the ranks of the clergy from those in their twenties to those in their forties these last years have been steadily thinned by the departure of men brought about by a whole series of factors, failures, even successes, but in which the canonical obligation of celibacy and the human need to marry are nearly always an important part of the story.

Celibacy made some sense within a wider and viable pattern of clerical life such as I have tried to delineate. That pattern has crumbled irretrievably in most Western countries, and the Vatican Council implicitly sanctioned its demise by all sorts of openings and exhortations, but without it compulsory celibacy for the diocesan clergy is simply not on. The attempt to main-tain celibacy by law outside its context is a key factor in the present disintegration of the Catholic clergy—and disintegration is not too strong a word for what is now taking place, much as authority tries to disguise the extent of the disaster.

It is impossible to find any sound doctrinal or theological reason for a general law of priestly celibacy. Today this is very much part of the practical difficulty: if people believe in its theoretical justification they may put up with great personal strain, but they are far less likely to do so when they feel that the underlying theory has been demolished, as it has. Probably even a majority of bishops are now coming to see this clearly enough, and it is hardly open to doubt that the law will be decisively changed within the next ten years—though again it is sadly probable that when the change is admitted, it will be initially carried out in such a clericalist and restrictive manner that the immediate consequence will be still further damage both to the existing body of clergy and to an appreciation of the true nature of the ministry. But nothing is done now at a cost of immense damage to the pastoral care of the whole Church, to the cause of a rational, pondered restructuring of the ministry in the light of Vatican II, and to the lives of thousands of priests caught willy-nilly in the new situation. Surely in this matter if in any Pope Paul carries a massive personal responsibility. Despite much advice to the contrary and a strong vote in favour of the ordination of married men at the third Synod, he has set himself inflexibly against any change in the matter and this personal decision is effectively strangling the ministry of the Church he has been set to watch over.

The twentieth-century Secretariat of State and its two out-standing papal representatives, Pius XII and Paul VI, see the Church's influence upon the wider world chiefly in terms of diplomacy, government and law. The Vatican is represented as a government, its nuncios and internuncios are part of the diplomatic corps in most countries—one of the most striking developments of these ten years being precisely the large increase in the number of such papal diplomats now at work up and down the world. It is through the permanent legal relationship of a concordat or the particular diplomatic intervention of a nuncio that the Secretariat of State sees the cause of Christ and his kingdom being advanced. This tends of necessity to be an exclusive approach. The diplomatic door will be closed if other approaches are used at the same time—such at least is the threat and the fear. Consequently, once the choice has been made that the Vicar of Christ should exercise his ministry to the world in all those areas of human concern which include some more or less political dimension as if he were a government, he is then prevented from approaching them in any other way. He cannot speak out; he cannot protest about injustice, torture and massacre in any except the vaguest and most enigmatic language; he can hardly offer comfort to those most in need of it. He has been caught within the self-deception of the governmental game. And this, of course, is what the governments of the world want of him. They are not moved by his diplomatic approaches, though they will throw him a sausage or two from time to time and even make his nuncio *doyen* of the diplomatic corps (what an achievement for the kingdom of God!), but they are frightened of his moral power, his voice with their people, his judgement upon their injustices. They would do a lot to gag him. In simpler ages they tried to gag the Pope with prison or exile. Today and for many decades they have gagged him far more effectively by accepting his accredited nuncios, signing his concordats, agreeing to play the whole absurd game of recognising the Vatican as a sovereign state—so long as he will not do what God has appointed him to do, speak out the truth without fear or favour.

All the agony of Pius XII's long failure to respond with clarity to the vast atrocities of Nazi tyranny—euthanasia, the genocide of the Jews, the mass murder of Poles and Russians—can only be understood in the light of the way that the Pope had been enslaved by his own system, the system of concordat and nunciature. He was, of course, also ensnared by his fear of Communism—and one had reason enough to fear Stalinism. But he was able to speak out adequately about the horrors of Stalinism as he never was about those of Nazism, not only because he recognised the evil of Communism while he was largely blind to that of Fascism, not only because of his personal fondness for Germany, but because in dealing with the Communist states he was not tied by his own self-imposed chains of concordat and nunciature.

This is not to say that the system of nuncios (or at least of Apostolic Delegates) does not have a valuable side to it. A wise nuncio may have a considerable beneficient influence, acting as a restraining brake upon the more tyrannical and unreasonable of local bishops. It is often said that the Apostolic Delegates in the United States exercised a certain liberalising influence upon the reactionary hierarchy of that country. Petty dictators may also pay considerably more respect to a nuncio than they would to a local archbishop, though major and more sophisticated dictators may use the nuncio to undermine the position of the local hierarchy. The system really becomes dangerous when a concordat is involved, particularly the sort of concordat which gives little privileges to the Church, and even not so little ones—a first class train ticket here: exemption from civil trial there; perhaps a salary for a bishop or a privileged grip upon religious instruction in state schools. At once the Church is tied; Rome is tied. Silence then becomes imperative lest these valuable plums be lost. We have seen in the last years how incapable the hierarchical church then becomes of challenging governmental tyranny in the case of Mozambique: the murder of Protestant pastors in prison; the wiping out of whole villages; the torture of catechists; the expulsion of the priests who were moved in agony of spirit to protest. Despite it all, neither the bishops (with one exception) dependent upon a regular subsidy from the state, nor Rome, grateful to the Portuguese government for removing all missionary expenses within its territories from the Church were able to do more than mouth almost unintelligible public regrets while making extremely ineffectual protests within the secrecy of the diplomatic forum. To such a condition has the papacy reduced itself by the regime of its Secretariat of State—and the power of the Secretariat of State has steadily grown in the curia these last ten years—indeed other departments, such as *Propaganda Fide*, have largely lost their traditional measure of independence, and the Pope himself is increasingly controlled and restricted in his knowledge by the faceless policy makers of the *Secretariat*.

Nobody expects the Church to be a decisive influence for good in countries where it is unrepresented or a very small minority. The quality of her influence can be better assessed in countries where Catholics form a majority. And here one must distinguish between its perennial influence at grass roots level and its more deliberate stance taken up at leadership level within the context of recent history. What did the Church ever do these last fifty years to enhance the sphere of freedom in Portugal and its overseas territories? That is a crucial question just because of the dominantly Catholic character of Portugal. Certainly Bishop Gomes of Oporto splendidly retrieved the situation by the quality of his own stance, but how much support did he get from the Patriarch of Lisbon or the Pope? Did not the institutional Church as a whole actually strengthen the oppressive regime, not only through the concordat but also through the steady stimulation of devotion at the shrine of Fatima, a devotion which subtly reinforced the political pattern of Salazarism? Pope Paul's visit to Fatima in May 1967 with all its curious interlocking of the devotional and the political was itself a major contribution to unfreedom in Portugal.

Italy and Ireland are two other examples where it is worth considering the effect of current official Catholicism. The concordat which Pius XI concluded with Mussolini, together with the traditional Catholic faith of the vast majority of Italians, have given the church a wholly exceptional position in Italy which, despite the very rapid decay of Italian Catholicism over the last fifteen years, it has not yet wholly lost. One need not question that much of the traditional religious spirit of the Italians—their easy but profound faith, strong devotions, cheerfulness, acceptance of the interlocking of natural and supernatural, loyalty to church and Pope—is one to be admired, even if it has long been combined with intellectual sterility, complacency with poverty and injustice, clerical privilege and anticlerical bitterness. But what has the Church contributed to helping the Italy of the last twenty years face up to the socio-moral problems of the modern world? One senses a terrible ethical aridity in Italian Catholicism, effectively tied as it has been to a single political party, *Democrazia Cristiana*, a force of some vigour in the late 1940s under De Gasperi but a party which could already be described in 1960 by a sympathetic observer as 'a ruling party worn down by years of uninterrupted tenure of power, of factional strife, of heavy and overt confessional pressures' (Richard Webster, *Christian Democracy in Italy*, p. 148). Fifteen years later, it has still never been out of office, a mentally and morally bankrupt symbol of official political Catholicism. While accepting the fall of Fascism, the Church in Italy could not really face the ups and downs of democratic change. Confronted by what, in the 1940s, was admittedly a very strong and militant Communist party, it felt compelled to play the power game and has been doing so ever since, despite Pope John's attempt to admit a somewhat wider sphere of political mobility for Catholics.

Here again, as in the international field, choosing one road of influence appears to have debarred the Church from choosing others. The mobilisation of a hierarchically directed Catholic Action to ensure the victory of the Christian Democrats has not only tied the Church to an increasingly corrupt and discredited establishment, it has also debarred it from a more detached and yet astringent approach to the needs of contemporary society, while guaranteeing that its own wealth and property ownership would not be called into question. Pollution, shanty towns, appalling town planning, the particularly disgusting state of the city of Rome, cholera, the decay of Venice, the Mafia, the decline of the south, hamstrung educational and medical systems—the list of Italy's current and crying social ills could be continued almost indefinitely, to say nothing of what has now become a state of almost continuous political paralysis. And where, amidst all these crucial human and social needs, has the Church exerted her weight? To prevent legal divorce and contraception. Really the mind boggles. When one considers the prevalence of abortion over the years in Italy, when one remembers the hundreds of thousands of Italians whose marriages have irretrievably broken down and who have for years been living with other people; when one considers the very restrained character of the divorce law against which the church's leaders were protesting, when one calls to mind all the other evils and abuses of society it was indeed a strange choice and the rebuff which the Italian people offered the Church in voting for divorce was a very well merited one. The whole episode, as so many others in the later years of Pope Paul's pontificate, shows a remarkable unawareness of the actual state of society—for it is not conceivable that the campaign for a referendum upon the divorce law would ever have got under way, if the Vatican had not wanted it and had not believed that it could succeed.

Let us turn to the very different situation of Ireland and its appalling conflict between 'Catholics' and 'Protestants' in the North. No one can reasonably suggest that this conflict is all or chiefly the fault of the Catholic Church. It is the culmination within the context of both the modern civil rights movement and the urban guerilla movement of a long history of colonialism, economic exploitation, religious persecution and oppression, tribal hostility, the sheer clash of cultures. The relevant question for Catholics qua Catholic is whether it is partly the fault of modern Catholicism; and when one asks that question one has first to recognise that, however much else it is, it is a conflict between adherents of Catholicism and of those of Protestantism operating with a renewed intensity of mutual fear and misunderstanding in a situation where many of the other forces which in the past produced the long feud are now well nigh spent. Neither the Catholic Church nor the Protestant Churches can of themselves solve today's conflict, but it would be a rash man who asserted that they cannot do a great deal more than they have done for reconciliation, or that they have not contributed and do not still contribute very considerably to producing and reinforcing the underlying causes behind the conflict.

Faced with this vast feud, what have they in fact done? One might expect them seriously to probe into the conduct of their ministries, the pattern of their organisation, the themes of their teaching, to see whether they are not in part to blame. Yet one hears little of such probing; what one has seen is the Church leaders come all together in complacent silliness to declare solemnly that it is not a sectarian conflict. In some sense that is so obviously true that it is not worth saying; in many others it is clearly not true. All that such a statement really means is an ignominious disclaimer of responsibility and in consequence a refusal either to be sorry for the past or to mend the future by changing their ways. And yet it is their ways which have done much to bring Ulster to its present pass.

This is not the place to examine the vast Protestant responsibility, the abysmal failure of the Anglican bishops of England over many years to raise their voices for justice in Northern Ireland, challenging this characteristic example of British colonial blindness; but it is the place to consider the ways whereby the Catholic Church, in all the weight of its official system, is gravely responsible.* The tragedy of modern Irish Catholicism is that it has carried across into a period of power and ecclesiastical wealth, the defensiveness, insistence upon the hard line, unconcern for the plight of the other side, natural to a period of oppression. And all this has confirmed Northern Protestants in their neurotic and largely unreasoning hostility to belonging to any state in which Catholics have political power. The conflict in the North is between two groups of people inhabiting the same land, sharing the same language, skin colour, Christian religion and much else, but divided by a quite fantastic gulf of blind group hostility. It is not an area division, nor a class division—though these factors clearly play some part in the overall picture. It is at its roots a tribal division, the tribal consciousness having been perpetuated principally through church allegiance and the activity of various fringe church organisations. In such a situation the primary social task of any church is to liberate people from such hostility; and such a task should take priority over every other social task. Such liberation can only be done through a multiplying of personal and social links between the two sides. Such links depend in any community very largely upon school and family connections. Yet the Catholic Church has taken a harder line—and continues today to take a harder line—against denominationally mixed schools and mixed marriages in Northern Ireland than almost anywhere else in the world. In doing so it makes a dubious appeal to 'divine law' which if valid would imply the condemnation of the church in many other parts of the world, and by reasserting its insistence upon these things in the present situation it is helping to ensure that the basic social conditions responsible for the conflict remain indefinitely.

When I visited Ballymurphy, one of the most deprived of the Catholic ghettoes of Belfast, a local Catholic doctor said to me: 'There are three forces which over the years have oppressed these people and reduced them to this state: one is Britain, the second is the Orange Order, and the third is the Catholic Church'. And looking at the vast and extremely expensive church which the ecclesiastical authorities had recently seen fit to erect in Bally-

---

* I do not consider here the ways in which British Catholics have gravely over the years evaded their responsibility in Irish matters (with the odd brave exception like Wilfred Scawen Blunt): half of them, so anxious not to appear Irish, steadily ignoring the deep and institutional injustices which Irish Catholics have suffered under the British crown; the other half, blinded by their Irish nationalist inheritance, terrifyingly insensitive to the reasonable rights and fears of Northern Protestants (though here too there have been some splendid exceptions). But in the end British Catholics are marginal to this question.

murphy (but which the local people, so many of them permanently out of work, would have to pay for) I did not find it difficult to see his point.

Recently a printed petition for the canonisation of Blessed Oliver Plunkett has been circulated in Ireland with the full support of the hierarchy. Plunkett was an archbishop and martyr in the seventeenth century and insistence upon his death is hardly likely to prove a reconciling attitude in present circumstances. I understand that in fact devotion to him is not very great in Ireland today. This, in fact, is an institutional ploy not a popular movement; but the petitions distributed through school children who are instructed to obtain the signatures of all at home and return them to the collectors, will then be piled up and presented in Rome 'to demonstrate beyond doubt' the desire of the Irish people for Plunkett's canonisation,* an event which can then be used very effectively as a rallying point for Irish-Catholic nationalism of the narrowest kind. The intrinsic significance of it shines out only too well from the prayer which goes with the petition: 'O God! We pray for peace and that Blessed Oliver Plunkett through whom you preserved the Catholic faith of the Irish people may soon be glorified by the honour of canonisation'. I quote this because it seems to me an excellent example of ecclesiastical double-talk. The non-committal prayer for peace is effectively nullified by the characteristic phrase 'the Catholic faith of the Irish people'—the very identification of being Irish with being Catholic, which is the reddest of all flags to the Ulster bull and really renders partition and the consequent communal conflict inevitable. Until the official Irish Catholic church ceases to equate being fully Irish and loyal to the tradition of Ireland with being Catholic and accepts that the Irish nation and tradition are pluriform, as are those of almost every other country, then there can be little hope for peace in the north.

Doubtless it is hard—just as it is hard for the Pope to agree to a mosque being built in Rome or for Spain to grant equal rights to Protestant churches. The temptation to identify church with state or church with people and to demand for your religion some sort of territorial or tribal absolutism has been very strong with Catholics. In yielding to it they cease to be Catholics and become instead tribalists and that, unfortunately, has been a very strong characteristic of modern Irish catholicism. A terrifying example of it was provided by an Irish priest who had worked for some thirty years in a South African diocese and made clear to me that,

* This has now been done and it has been announced (December 1974) that Plunkett will be canonised during the Holy Year.

though there were thousands of blacks in his parish, he was simply not interested in doing anything for them. When I asked why, he replied indignantly, 'Do you know, father, that there are people in this town with the name of Kelly, O'Reilly and O'Donovan who are not Catholics but Protestants. While there is a single person with Irish blood here who is not a Catholic, I will not turn to the Africans.' That is a true story and while doubtless an extreme case it does express a type of religious tribalism which is only too common in the Catholic Church and particularly within the Irish diaspora. It is surely far more forgivable there than in many other places, just because that intimate identification between Catholic church and Irishness was a truly supporting, and therefore liberating, influence upon poor Irishmen emigrating across the world with very little to support and comfort them; such an identification was far more genuinely Christian than comparable ones linking dominating and oppressive nations, such as the English and the French, with some version of christianity. Nevertheless it was finally mistaken and becomes dangerous indeed, when—as I have suggested—the oppression mostly disappears but the attitudes which it engendered remain. By and large Irishmen in South Africa and Boston are today very much part of the oppressing class despite their continued sense of Irish/Catholic identity. And even where the oppression does continue in some quite real form, that is to say in Northern Ireland, this species of ecclesiastical tribalism, while providing a rather phoney kind of consolation to the underdog, is in fact stimulating the oppression and the conflict. Until Irishmen cease to think that they have a prior right to call themselves Catholics, and Catholics in Ireland cease to think they have a prior right to call themselves Irishmen, the basic cultural and psychological ground for conflict will remain.

Certainly there are many Irish Catholics who see all this with absolute clarity today; what is significant, however, is that the Church's leadership continues to foster the myth of tribal/religious identity, just as it continues to insist upon regulations relating to marriage and schooling which are essentially oppressive for both sides because, within a society which is being literally destroyed by a particular pattern of division, these regulations accentuate that division. No one need doubt Irish Church leaders are sincere in their horror of violence and their appeals for peace but if such appeals wholly avoid the ways in which the churches have themselves substantially contributed to bringing ordinary Ulstermen to such a psychological pass that they bomb and shoot their neighbours, then they are an inadequate response to the situation.

The old Roman imperial formula for keeping the people happy was that of bread and circuses. The more modern papal one has been that of indulgences and canonisations. While indulgences are slowly slipping away from the Catholic consciousness despite papal attempts to retain them in a duly updated form, canonisations go on as an important part of the papal system of government. In principle and in origin nothing was more proper and congruent with the Christian spirit than to recognise after death the exceptional holiness of certain members of the Church and to respect and imitate them accordingly. It has been an almost instinctive movement of Christian people in every age and land, and a most fruitful one. What is alarming is the political and administrative character of the modern canonisation. The long process and careful regulations developed over the ages did have their point even if they were too much a part of the wider movement of Roman centralisation: some discipline in regard to the recognition of a saint was necessary as some control over the way veneration was subsequently expressed. Nevertheless in fact the control developed in Rome itself admitted, indeed produced, horrid abuses in the whole business—such as, in our time, the slow cutting up of the dead body of Maria Goretti for distribution as tiny particles of relic all over the world. But what of late years is particularly alarming is the increasing tendency to short circuit due processes and bring about a rapid canonisation which will somehow validate this cause or that. It is true that one aspect of the process which can almost never be short-circuited is the financial. I know of one procurator general of a missionary society who resigned rather than pay the sums required in a canonisation process on which his society was set. Without such payments the cause will not make due progress. It is said that one of the biggest religious bodies in the world puts aside, or until recently put aside, a regular proportion of its general income to advance the canonisations of its members, considering that such canonisations make an important contribution to its public image. It is clear that if a country or its hierarchy wants some of its own ecclesiastical heroes canonised, it must find a very considerable sum. A refusal to play such games and lack of money is doubtless one big reason why no Carthusian, despite the intense spirituality of that order, has been canonised for many hundreds of years, other than those included with the English Reformation martyrs.

What is still more serious, however, is the move towards canonising figures whose ecclesiastical politics and legacy are now being called in question. It can be a powerful way of impeding that questioning among Catholics. Pius X's canonisation by Pius XII was also in a way canonisation of his very tough treatment of the modernists. Pius IX's cause has been under consideration for many years but here even the most ardent advocates of canonising popes (the conferring of a sort of extended post mortem infallibility) have had their doubts. There is now a very real possibility that Paul VI will canonise Pius XII. This would most certainly mean the abandonment of any pretence at following the normal process of canonisation and could only be seen as a stridently political action: an attempt to rule out of court Catholic critics of Pius XII and what he stood for. This is all the more serious when one considers not only the very large scale questioning of Pope Pius' role in the Nazi period, but also the close personal relationship which existed between him and Mgr Montini and the extent to which the one has been successor to the other, not simply as bishop of Rome but as exponent of that view of the Church seen from the Secretariat of State.

The central disaster of these years remains, however, that related to the encyclical on birth control entitled *Humanae Vitae* and published in 1968. The seriousness of that issue was not accidental nor related to a merely ecclesiastical criterion of significance, the significance of the crisis over *Humanae Vitae* basically derived from the fact that the development of a thoroughly responsible attitude to human population increase is probably the most serious issue facing the whole world today. No single document has done more to confuse and corrupt the Church than this. The basically correct traditional Christian judgement that in a society of high infant mortality and low population increase contraceptive practices were selfish and immoral has been transposed across a spurious natural law ethic tied far too closely to precise physical actions into a society of overall low infant mortality and high population increase to produce a papal ruling evidently impractical and rejected by the moral good sense of Christian and non-Christian alike.

We have now the absurd position in the Catholic Church of, on the one hand, Rome officially maintaining the clear, unambiguous line of *Humanae Vitae*, supported in this by its nuncios and a number of hierarchies such as the Irish and, to a lesser extent, the British, and attempting to suppress any other expression of Catholic opinion in public. On the other hand we have, not only scores of theologians and millions of devoted practising lay married Catholics, but also the quietly formulated but quite clearly different teaching of a large number of hierarchies: 'A Christian, in order to form his moral judgement, will always give proper and full consideration to the position of the Holy Father. However, it is also understood and agreed upon that parents, in consideration of the need to strengthen the love between themselves and the needs of their family, will perhaps in special circumstances arrive at a conclusion contrary to the teachings of the encyclical.' (The Bishops of Indonesia, 1968. They issued a further, still clearer and more general statement on the matter in August 1973. Many hierarchies throughout the world have published statements in the same sense.)

Humanae Vitae has intensely confused the Church both at the level of personal pastoral ministry and that of an effective social policy. Fifty years ago the regular Catholic teaching was that a good Christian couple would have as many children as God gave them, full stop. But this is not the teaching today. The Vatican Council fully accepted that people have a grave personal responsibility to decide for themselves how many children they should have. This was a major revolution and it shows that Catholic moral teaching can and does develop. What it stuck at was the relatively trivial question of means. At present the Roman view only allows absolute continence or the 'rhythm method'. It is perfectly clear that the former can be disastrous for a marriage and even St Paul is hesitant about encouraging it, while the latter simply does not work with some people while it is far too complicated for use in most of the poorer and more illiterate societies of the world. The great majority of women in this world can still hardly read or write and they can't afford thermometers. What the church is, then, officially saying to the majority of the people in the world today is this: 'God the all powerful and all wise very much wants you to limit your family, but he has unfortunately given you no practical way in which to do so. Man has found various ways in which you can fulfil God's intention, but we have to tell you that God has forbidden you to make use of any of these ways'. What greater nonsense can one imagine! A nonsense which derives from a primitivistic conception of what is 'naturally' good and human.

Quite apart from the wider issues of population increase there are millions of married people in the world who have very good personal reasons for not having another child: the health of the mother, poverty and a large family, lack of accommodation ... Fortunately, even in Britain and Ireland, priests are increasingly advising one thing to such people in private and saying another to their bishops. It is good that people should all the same be helped—so long as they choose a wise confessor, if indeed they still have enough confidence to go to any at all—but it is appalling that the Church should be corrupted by this vast non-conformity between the practice of the laity and the advice of many clergy upon one side, the 'official' line upon the other. And it is yet another reason why priests, ashamed of the double talk involved, give up their ministry.

The vast population increase in the world at large is not only a major social problem for us all, it is already a decisive factor in some crisis situations such as those of the Sahel and Bangla Desh; in the coming decades it will weigh in an ever heavier manner upon more and more areas of the world. A serious moral approach to it is quite impossible with a blanket condemnation of contraception, and the effective consequence of *Humanae Vitae* is to exclude Catholics officially from struggling with these central issues of the human future. We are tied down, instead, to an endless dreary, half-suppressed debate about trivia.

One further important consequence of this is that it has largely ruled Catholic opposition to abortion out of court in the eyes of the wider world. Contraception and abortion are very different things—one is an essentially non-moral matter, the other can be a way of killing people—but the more difficult it is to practise contraception the more abortion there will surely be. It is no accident that abortion rates in Italy are terrifyingly high, and the Catholic Church does not even seem to mind, so long as there is no legal acceptance. It has become clear as day that the campaign against easy abortion is crippled by the rejection of contraception. Here as over the wider population issue it is tragic that the possibility of positive moral witness on major matters has been gravely damaged by the false stance taken up by *Humanae Vitae*.

Finally, there is no matter which has more gravely weakened the authority of the papacy itself. The ministries of the Church can be misused but if they are their proper authority is bound to be damaged. *Humanae Vitae* has succeeded in doing this to a quite terrifying extent, contributing to a deep cynicism about both pope and bishops and producing the impression that Rome does not even much care what is actually done or not done by the laity, so long as its authority is not ostensibly challenged by the clergy. It is a sad day for those of us who do still believe profoundly in the petrine ministry.

What ever way one turns one sees today an extraordinary contrast between the hard official line coming from Rome and what is actually happening: refusal to allow a married clergy contrasted with what can only be described as a vast loss of faith in the value of compulsory celibacy upon the part of the clergy themselves, and a steady fall in numbers; the clinging on to concordats with

Spain, Portugal and Italy contrasted with the bitter rejection of the whole concordat arrangement by more and more people inside these countries and the desperate appeal of a man like the bishop of Nampula for an end to the concordat and all that has gone with it. To such an appeal the ears of Rome are deaf. *Humanae Vitae* upon one side, the practice of married Catholics all over the world on the other. The hard line against civil divorce in Italy, its massive acceptance by Italians, most of whom are at least nominal Catholics. Attempt after attempt to prevent growth of sharing in eucharistic communion on one hand, the steady advance of intercommunion upon the other.

It is at times difficult to understand how the Pope and his curial advisers can be so out of touch with the signs of the times as they appear today, retreating into political conservatism, other-worldly spirituality and the persecution of clerical dissent—Dom Franzoni and Hans Kung above all. The lamentable story of the ill-treatment of Franzoni, one time abbot of St Paul's and luminary of the church of Rome, will surely constitute in itself in the sight of history one of the heaviest indictments of papal rule in these years. Even when one can point to a memorable achievement of Pope Paul from his earlier years, such as the 1967 encyclical *Populorum Progressio* upon social development, the practical follow-up has been inhibited, not only by the implications of *Humanae Vitae*, but also by the Roman insistence on playing the development game at the level of government and diplomacy rather than at the level of church and gospel (hence the debacle a few years ago over the ecumenical development agency SODEPAX and its defusing after a splendid start into a rather innocuous organisation which would not embarrass the Secretariat of State in its diplomatic relations).

Must one, then, take a wholly pessimistic view of the Catholic Church in the post-Vatican II era? By no means. The people of God are far from wholly dependent upon the hierarchy. It is not only that many of the documents of the Council did start a process of renewing the body which nothing can stop—in worship and prayer, in the service of the wider community, in ecumenical relations, in scholarship and theology. It is that with the steady declericalisation of the Church, an ever larger number of people are consciously and conscientiously bearing the weight of the Church's ministry—the communication of the word of God, the service of neighbour, the building up of the Christian fellowship. Again, if Europe hesitates, South America, Africa and Asia go from strength to strength, as the 1974 Synod so well showed. The balance of ecclesial geography is changing and the very mediocrity of European ecclesiastical leadership in these years is enabling this very proper change of balance to come about more easily. What Rome does, what the bishops do, matter less and less.

If God is not with us then indeed we are the most unfortunate of people; but if God is as we believe him to be, then we need not fear the most mediocre and misguided leadership the Church has had to suffer for many years. There have been many times within the history of the Church when one could only look at the papacy with horror, such was its worldliness, the crimes associated with its court. Yet the Church survived. Today this is not the case. We are blessed with a Pope intensely sincere, conscientious, devout, personally gentle, a person whom one cannot but revere. If, an old man, caught in the bonds of his curial past and curial present, misled by the monsignori of the Secretariat of State, he has failed objectively upon issue after issue to lead us forward with confidence, humour and insight, then we have all the same to thank our heavenly Father for all his gifts—both for the help he offers and for that which he appears to withhold—and in a time of marked leaderlessness to turn to him in faith and hope and to persevere lovingly in the Church of our calling. There is no other way.

5

A typology of church-state relations

The relations of church and state provide one of the richest themes in the cultural history of Europe—from the stark 'non licet esse christianus' of the early Roman Empire to the imprisonment or deportation of church leaders in several countries and continents during the last years. St Ambrose turning the Emperor Theodosius from the cathedral of Milan; Charles the Great crowned by the Pope and scores of kings and emperors after him anointed and crowned by Popes and bishops; Henry IV waiting humiliated before Canossa; Boniface VIII struck in the face at Anagni; Henry II struggling with Thomas Becket; Henry VIII executing John Fisher; church courts and the constitutions of Clarendon and Provisions and Praemunire, establishment and disestablishment, kulturkampf and concordat, the extirpation of the Albigensians, the burning of Huss, the curbing of Anabaptists and fifth monarch men, from Pope and Emperor to squire and parson—the subject is unending in the wealth of its issues, the diversity of its patterns, the seriousness and at times the majesty of its participants. It is fascinating when one turns to the history of modern Africa to see so many different and significant patterns and issues emerging here too within the field of church-state relations. One can imagine in Europe, certainly naively, that the area of church-state relations has become today a limited and uncontroversial one apart from minor constitutional details or a tussle in a pre-modern backwater such as Northern Ireland or Franco's Spain. But in contemporary Africa, as in South America and Asia, it is plainly a topic of quite central importance in many different countries, even if it is one about which very little has hitherto been written.

If we are to grow in the understanding of it, the first need would seem to be a realisation that today as in past church history there is much complexity in the issues involved and a very great diversity between actually existing situations. My intention here is to attempt a pragmatic outline for a typology of these relations, of the issues involved, and of the deciding factors which make in one situation and another for tension and conflict or for harmony and co-operation, with some particular reference to contemporary Africa.

The ground for every relationship between church and state is the area of their overlapping. This area may be larger or smaller but it always exists. It exists in people themselves because wherever there is a church (a religious society not forming part of another religious society)[1] its membership is shared with that of the state. People who are in one are also in the other. But it is in the nature of each to claim some form of absolute loyalty, though this may be more or less pressed in different circumstances. In traditional scholastic terminology the two are 'perfect societies', by which it was meant that in its own line each was a whole, not part of or dependent upon some larger body, and could make correspondingly absolute claims: the state as regards the 'common good' of its citizens in time and space, the church as regards the eternal spiritual good of its members. In some way each lays claim to an absoluteness in importance, a constitutional inability to be rightly over-ridden by anything else. This seems to be of the deep nature both of the state and of religion (and religion's sociological incarnation—the church), though in many circumstances such claims will not be over-sharply formulated or pressed in practice. Now, although the Church's absoluteness may be in relation to God, to 'the next world' or to 'spiritual things', in fact it exists in this world, claims this world to be God's world and somehow subject to his laws; whatever authority it has, has to be exercised here—ordering human behaviour here in relation to God or the kingdom of heaven: some ways of behaviour are mandatory for its members if they are to 'do God's Will', be 'good Christians' or whatever, and some ways of behaviour must be outlawed for the same reasons. At times it may be more a matter of a general line of encouragement or discouragement than of direct positive or negative command. In practice there may be a greater or lesser likelihood of such norms clashing with other sets of norms formulated by the state or wider policies encouraged by the state, but such a possibility always exists.

Alternatively, it may be that the norms generated by the two societies coincide or correspond to a significant extent, and that

[1]The category of church is used in this paper to cover non-Christian religious societies as well as Christian ones, but the development of its argument relates for the most part to Christian bodies.

each side banks upon this correspondence and the mutual support it brings about. The church may stress the duty of civil obedience as a man's prime social obligation: the state, far from resenting such ecclesiastical interference in the political system, welcomes it as reinforcing its own norms with an additional religious sanction. The over-lap of area between church and state is here not only not resented but is taken as providing a needed religious basis for the state as well as civil recognition for the church: it is the ground for co-operation and mutual support as, in different circumstances, it is the ground for conflict or mutual distrust.

The over-lap always exists but occasionally it is not recognised —the state simply ignores the church and the church ignores the state. In practice this seems possible only when churches are very small in proportion to the state. Elsewhere the over-lap exists and is recognised to exist, but its treatment and consequences vary according to types of society, of state and of church, and these provide us with a vast range of very different patterns for church-state relations.

In the construction of an over-all typology of these relations we will therefore consider six things. The first is the various basic patterns of relationship possible; the second, an analysis of types of church in relation to the state; the third, types of state in relation to the church; the fourth, deeper elements in the shape of society which can influence both state and church; the fifth, the grounds of co-operation; the sixth, the grounds of conflict.

Basically there are five possible patterns for church-state relations and it is well to begin by outlining them.

1. The state ignores the church or churches, either because they are so small as to be insignificant or because it is determinedly secularist. They may have some legal existence as private associations but the state avoids any recognition that they have a sphere or competence proper to them.

2. The state proscribes the church and persecutes its members or at least discriminates against them. The church is here seen as a rival or as a subversive or anti-national influence. This is frequently the case when the state is in fact linked with another church, religion or comparable ideology which claims a monopoly or which has given the state a certain character with which the persecuted church appears incompatible. It can also be the case in reaction to a period of strong church influence over the state or when the proscribed church is seen as associated with a foreign and threatening power.

3. The state clearly co-operates with the church or churches in certain more or less important areas; there is some public recognition of their existence, a willingness to share work in definite fields, but certainly no identification and possibly a touchiness on either side if the other appears to be encroaching beyond what is seen as its proper sphere. This is often the pattern where there are a number of churches of some size within one state.

4. The state gives privilege to the church and a special status in society; it 'establishes' the church. The state probably supports it financially, it may limit teaching opposed to its doctrines, it possibly penalises citizens who are not church members. It may even claim that there should be identity of membership between church and state. At the same time the state clearly controls the church in many important ways and may appoint its senior ministers or indeed all of them. The situation of the Church of England from Elizabeth I to the twentieth century illustrates this pattern.

5. This is similar in many ways to the fourth pattern, but in it the Church not the state retains ultimate control of both—as in Calvin's Geneva, the papal states, or even, to some extent, medieval Europe after the Gregorian Reform and before the fourteenth century. In some cases it may be really impossible to distinguish between **(4)** and **(5)**: the symbiosis of church and state has become such that one can hardly declare that one controls the other: they are near to being a single organic whole. One could think of tenth-century England, but even more—in a non-christian context—of traditional African society.

Each of these patterns can, of course, be modified in various ways—there are many degrees of persecution, of co-operation and of establishment. Moreover one pattern may fade with time into another. Thus the establishment of the Church of England has slowly been eroded so that the present state/Church of England relationship in England, while remaining legally inside the fourth category, is really getting nearer and nearer to the third. The relations between the Roman Catholic Church and the British state between the seventeenth and twentieth century moved slowly from various forms of **(2)**, through **(1)** to **(3)**. Today millions of pounds of British government money are devoted to the building and running of Catholic church schools. In other cases a pattern of complete ignoring slowly melts into a mild form of recognition and co-operation, often in the case of very small churches. But the basic division remains.

It covers, however, vast differences between the real situation of cases included within a single category. We need now to clarify these differences further and at the same time analyse the factors which in a given country explain why church-state relations take a particular form. To do this we must consider each of the three elements involved separately: that is to say, the church, the state, and the area of common ground.

It would be naive to think that from our viewpoint all churches are really much the same or are looking for the same things. Churches differ significantly between themselves and even within themselves from one age or region to another. Which elements within the doctrine and life and ethos of a church, we have now to ask, are significant in affecting a typology of church-state relations?

I suggest that we can usefully classify churches for this purpose according to four different criteria: **(i)** size: **(ii)** a this worldly as against an other worldly emphasis: **(iii)** attitudes towards other churches and religions: **(iv)** ecclesiastical organisation. Inevitably there must be some over-simplification in attempting to categorise complex and subtle organisms, each with its own characteristic web of doctrine, theology and ecclesiastical life in these or any ways, but they are, I believe, valid and useful categories even if—when applied to particular cases—they inevitably need to be further nuanced.

i. Size. This is best measured in numerical relation with that of the state and is undoubtedly of great import in shaping the pattern of church-state relations. So as not to over-complicate matters we can best limit our consideration to three different sizes. **(a)** the very small church, under 5% of the population of the state and often much less: **(b)** the substantial minority church, 5% to 40% of the population: **(c)** the majority church, at times including at least nominally over 90% of the general population—in Africa this latter is only true of certain Northern Islamic countries. In practice the pattern of church/state relations differs greatly in these three cases. In the first case the pattern generally veers between **(1)** and **(2)**—ignoring and tension. The state can expect little help from such churches and will generally give little in return; but it may be suspicious of them just because they aren't well known and often flourish among some under-privileged section of society. They may be new arrivals and small young churches tend to take their doctrines more literally and be less accommodating than old and big ones.

Middle sized churches can seldom be effectively persecuted for long, but they can also hardly be established. The state inevitably tends to see them as stable bodies of respectable citizens with a useful social potential and relations with them tend to fall into category **(3)**, but the case may be rather different if their strength is wholly or chiefly related to a particular district or group of

51

citizens already somewhat apart. In which case they may be viewed with more suspicion: as in nineteenth-century Britain where the large Catholic population was nearly all in Ireland, or the Sudan with its strong Christian element in the south, or certain Moslem areas of the Philippines.

Where one church has the great majority of citizens as its members, there will either be a very large measure of amalgamation between the two and of dependence one upon the other, or some degree of tension. In the modern world in many places where the church is not now established, it used to be or to have far greater legal privileges than it now enjoys, and in some places present relations are still affected by memories of the past: fears of a recrudescence of clerical power, suspicion of any ecclesiastical influence in the political, and so forth. In contemporary Africa we have a number of instances of a majority church, or of churches which have somehow seen themselves as possessing this role. There is the position of Islam in Somalia, the Sudan, and other northern states; there is the state church of Ethiopia—not in fact numerically predominant in the country as a whole, but clearly established and privileged; there was the position of the Catholic Church in the Portuguese territories, very far from being in fact the church of the majority, but with all the privileges and intimate government involvement of an established church granted by the colonial power as an extension of the religious position inside Portugal; there is the very interesting situation in Zaire—the size of the Catholic Church there (nearly half of the whole population) with its fifty dioceses and great past privileges and power in the colonial period has created a situation in which the resultant tension is somewhat similar to some situations known in European Latin countries or, again, in South America; the position of the Catholic Church in Rwanda and Burundi is comparable; finally, there is South Africa in which the Dutch reformed Church has claimed something of the status of a majority church.

Majority churches could, perhaps, be best divided into two sub-groups: in one (i) are those with up to some 75% of the population, while the other (ii) can be typified by the church with some 95% of the population as its members. These two situations are really very different but they are often confounded, and their identification can cause much trouble. To take an example: the Roman Catholic church is some 70% of the population of the whole of Ireland but 95% of the Republic of Ireland. The relationship to the state of a church which does not include 30% of a nation's population must be significantly different from that of one which only fails to include 5%. Yet an important element in

Ireland's psychological problem has been the failure of many Irish Catholics to distinguish adequately between the two. In Ethiopia the traditional identification of the state with the Orthodox 'majority', to the exclusion of Moslems and others, may be an even clearer example of misinterpretation of the proper status for a majority of the first type.

ii Every church will teach about man's duties in the present world in relation to a coming world. However, the type of duty most stressed and the balance of concern between the two worlds can vary greatly. With some over-simplification one can properly contrast an 'other-worldly' teaching (d) with a 'this-worldly' teaching (e). The former will stress that reward comes after death, that this life is a 'vale of tears', that the Christian's duty is to bear the cross, that God has set each person in his state in life, that the only thing which finally matters is a holy death. The Church's action will concentrate upon inculcating attitudes of resignation, obedience and asceticism, upon providing the spiritual support of the sacraments, upon encouraging attendance at worship.

This attitude may be carried a stage further in some forms of immediate millennialism—the belief that this world is rapidly to pass away, probably in a matter of a few years, and be replaced by the kingdom of God; hence quite ordinary activities such as working for one's living, paying taxes, and marrying may be rejected as pointless or wrong in present circumstances. Comparable conclusions may be derived from 'gnostic' beliefs about the evilness of material things, materiality being seen as the chief characteristic of the present world. The two worlds are not then seen as one leading to the other, but in direct opposition: the duty of the religious man finding himself in this present world is immediately to withdraw from it so far as he can.

In contrast a 'this-worldly' church will stress the Christian's duty of working for the manifestation of the kingdom of God upon earth through the full round of human life, of showing one's religious commitment by participation in all sides of life, including the political. God is not satisfied with temple sacrifices but with care for the widow, the orphan and the stranger. Just as the one view, at its extremity, urges the religious man to opt out even of marriage and the normal duties of family life, so the other view urges the religious man to participate not only in married life but also in community and political life.

It is clear enough that if the first group of attitudes is dominant in a church, it will be able to co-operate well with certain political regimes but may be regarded as unhelpful by others, as, for instance, merely reinforcing the fatalism and passivity of people. If, on the contrary, it takes the second point of view, it is likely to clash strongly with some governments, but its influence will be welcomed by others. The first type was encouraged in Portugal, tolerated even in the USSR and regarded as the proper function of religion by dominant circles in South Africa; the second type may well come to clash from time to time with almost any government but particularly with those more clearly involved in oppression or discrimination against one race or group of people.

It should be noted here that the distinction between 'other-worldly' and 'this-worldly' teaching is not as such at all the same as one between life styles, particularly the life styles of church leaders. While certain extreme types of teaching almost must be noticeably reflected in life style, more diffuse teaching can in fact get away with a life style not obviously appropriate. Thus 'other-worldly' teaching, while it may be coupled with an ascetical life style, often goes the other way, at least in church leaders: a rich church closely linked with the powers of this world and very much enjoying the good things of life, offers a clearly 'other-worldly' gospel (particularly, of course, to its poorer members). Equally a 'this-worldly' gospel may also go with a this-worldly life style, but it may well not: a this-worldly gospel and asceticism is as possible an option as an other-worldly gospel coupled with a bishop's palace and a seat in the House of Lords. It might, in this context, be helpful to develop a contrast between the sort of asceticism which goes with an other-worldly gospel and the sort which goes with a this-worldly one.

(iii) A church's theological sense of itself in relation to other religious bodies can again have important consequences for church-state relations, at least if it is big enough to be able to influence public policy either directly or through the actions of its members.

On the one side we have (f) a church which considers itself to be the exclusive ark of salvation; it may go so far as to say that all non-members are damned. It has the truth, those who disagree with it are in error and error has no rights. The church as established by God has a right to the state's active support because the state's authority also comes from God; other churches, on the contrary, should receive no support from the state and should perhaps further be deprived of any public channel for propagating their doctrines: permission to propagate false doctrine is not liberty but licence.

On the other side (g) we have a church which stresses that all worth-while human actions must be done in freedom, which is finally a greater gift than authority; it must not be taken away in the religious sphere by any form of coercion. God will judge men on what was humanly possible for them and while establishing a church to speak with his authority, offers his grace and truth through other channels as well. The church as a body of human beings has many faults and much to repent, while because God works also in other bodies, they also have their contribution to offer. The church claims only the right to witness and to serve, not to compel or to dominate.

If a majority church takes by and large the first attitude, it will endeavour to create a relationship of religious privilege for itself with the state and this may gravely affect the relations between the state and other small churches in an adverse manner; while if it takes the second point of view, it may even do its best to ensure that the rights of small churches are respected equally with its own.

(iv) Our final contrast in church typologies concerns the shape of the ecclesiastical structure. Again to over-simplify we can take as one model a church (h) in which all authority to teach and rule comes from above, in which lay members are expected to keep their place and to listen attentively. Docility is their prime virtue. The Church's position on any given matter will be made clear by its leaders—the bishops or others; once that has been done, it is the duty of the faithful to give them all possible obedience and support.

We can compare this with a model (i) in which the church is seen primarily as the whole body of believers, in which the ministers may be elected, and in which it is expected that different members will receive different gifts. While the ordained ministry may be expected to preach and administer the sacraments, others may well provide the leadership for other areas of church life, and such leadership may evolve in a variety of ways.

On the whole, the first pattern of church life is likely to find itself at ease within a constitutionally authoritarian state, and the second pattern within a democratic state; and churches have in fact mostly evolved in this way—their governmental pattern either reflecting or influencing that of the country in which they exist. A similarity of organisational structure between church and state does not, however, rule out conflict: democratic churches can clash with democratic states and authoritarian churches can certainly clash with authoritarian states. But the shape of a conflict between an authoritarian church and an authoritarian state will be different from that between a democratic church and an authoritarian state, or an authoritarian church and a democratic state. The more 'democratic' be the form of the church, the more likely it is that church-state conflict will cease to be a straight clash between the leaders of the two bodies and tend instead to take the form of the political action of committed Christians acting on their own or in fairly small groups; this is above all the case where the state too is democratic.

It is to be remembered that these characteristics as outlined in **ii**, **iii** and **iv** can all be found in small, medium and majority churches. Further, they can be combined in a variety of ways. One could agree that a traditional Roman Catholic pattern provides one extreme type, combining **a**, **d**, **f**, and **h**—a majority church, strongly hierarchical, other-worldly and exclusive; but 'other-worldliness' is a particularly complex and varied characteristic and it could be claimed that the traditional Catholic pattern, while admittedly hierarchical and exclusive, had a strong tinge of 'this-worldliness' about it—far more so than either the Greek Orthodox or some Protestant traditions. Certainly today it could be argued that the Catholic tendency in each case is towards the poles of **e**, **g** and **i**: this-worldly, ecumenical and democratic, though the distance achieved may vary; the present tendency in many Anglican and Protestant churches is the same, though many Anglican dioceses still tend to the hierarchical and the other-worldly, though not to the exclusive. **d**, **g** and **h** is a fairly common Anglican pattern. A common Protestant pattern on the other hand, has been **d**, **f** and **i**: democratic, 'other-worldly' and exclusive. This may be particularly true of some very small churches.

Again, it could be demonstrated that churches shift quite rapidly back and forwards from an other-worldly to a this-worldly emphasis, particularly as the contrast between the two, as also between **f** and **g**, is not so much a matter of basic doctrine as of theological interpretation and spiritual emphasis. Hence it is possible for both attitudes to be held at the same time in the same church, and this indeed is often the case today. Elements within one church may hold strongly to both **d** and **f**, while other elements will hold equally strongly to attitudes which can be included under **e** and **g**. A church may well be polarised on these lines from within and as a consequence part of it may find it quite easy to co-operate with a particular government, while another section of it is in almost open conflict.

In general extreme other-worldliness (e.g. millennialism) and strong this-worldliness would seem likely to have political implications and hence stimulate church-state tension: moderate other-worldliness is what the state probably hopes for if it does not want the church to be troublesome or socially and politically influential.

Our typology of churches has hitherto considered them as entities entirely bounded by a given state. This is true of some but is clearly not true of others. A further, fifth, dimension has therefore to be added: the church with major external connections (j1) and the church without them (j2). A church which is small here may be big and influential elsewhere, and its over-all policy may be largely decided elsewhere; this is clearly particularly true of a rather centralised international church such as the Roman Catholic with its system of nuncios appointed to governments in most parts of the world but responsible to the Secretariat of State in Rome. The Catholic Church is very small in Somalia, medium size in South Africa, a majority church in Rwanda, but its image and policy is to a considerable extent (though far from entirely) the same everywhere. Yet, though this dimension is not to be ignored, it seems seldom to be the decisive one for long; even within the Roman Catholic communion, different national branches of the church in fact vary enormously in social and political attitude, responding to a certain national tradition and situation.

What is normally decisive in church-state relations is rather the overall character of this regional or national branch of a church than its wider world character—though the latter may on occasion impinge upon the former in no uncertain manner. It impinges particularly in Africa where most of the churches are relatively young and tend still to be somewhat dependent upon the source church from which they sprang for personnel, money and theology. This is, again, particularly true of the Catholic church: in almost every African country a majority of Catholic priests are foreigners, bringing with them their own attitudes in regard to church priorities, the proper approach to the state and so forth. Clearly this greatly increases the influence of the world church upon the local church. This dimension is indeed one of those which give church situations in Africa their most specific character. Although some churches are entirely indigenous, the large majority of Christians in Africa belong to churches which either still depend to a very considerable degree upon churches outside Africa or until recently have so depended; the pattern of church-state relationships either in colonial or in post-colonial times has been very significantly affected by this dependence. While this is doubtless diminishing considerably as the years pass, it will be long before a serious element of colonialism (or neocolonialism), with its consequent assets and weaknesses, can be discarded as irrelevant to the current character of the main mission-founded churches.

We turn now to the second element in the relationship: the state. It is even more difficult to provide an adequate typology of the state in relation to the church than it is of the church in relation to the state, and what I offer here is very tentative.

First, a state may or may not be in principle secularist. A non-secular state (k) is committed to some church, religion or 'religious ideology' (e.g. atheistic Marxism). In this case it is bound to favour the church or religious or ideological group which incorporates its own religious commitment, probably by some form of 'establishment' and either to ban other churches or to discriminate, to a greater or lesser degree, against them. The secular state (l) of its nature does not admit such a commitment and is able to consider different churches and religions on an equal, if perhaps uniformly unfavourable, basis. A state in principle secular may of course discriminate against a particular church as a consequence of past history or the prejudices of the majority of its citizens, or it may to some extent discriminate against all churches because the nature of its secularism—without committing it to some other positive ideology—is nevertheless markedly anti-religious. Anti-ecclesiasticism was probably more a characteristic of nineteenth-century secularism than it is of that of today. It is noticeable that the great majority of recently independent African countries have taken in principle a secular stance, unlike many of the countries of Asia. This secularism has in general, however, no anti-religious character. Constitutionally Africa today may be the most secular of continents despite the clear importance that religion has in the life of many people; only in the North have some countries maintained a specific religious (Islamic) commitment while Ethiopia has an official Christian character. Nevertheless this modern African secularity is clearly not pressed. Public occasions often begin with prayers of an ecumenical or inter-religious kind and it could be argued that a state such as Zambia has at present a fairly definite Christian complexion.

A second issue for our typology of the state is whether or not it is basically what we may call democratic (m) or what we may call authoritarian (n). This is clearly a matter of degree and is no easy thing to gauge. The decisive issue here is not so much the character of its legislative system and elections as whether in some form it admits of public opposition, disagreement with the government, the criticism of a moderately free press, and structures of society—educational, professional and philanthropic—not closely controlled by the state. To the extent that it does, an independent voice from the church can be fitted into the wider pattern of public life; where it does not, church criticism tends at once to be treated as seditious. As many consider it to be a prime task of the church to be a spokesman for morality and to denounce grave wrongs, particularly when committed by the powerful, the exercise of this task will result quite differently in democratic and non-democratic countries. In the former such activity will not usually result in any particular church-state confrontation, it will simply become part of the wider public dialogue and may influence voters in elections; in the second such activity will either, because of the power of the established church within the system, bring about a favourable response from the government, or it can bring church and state into head-on collision.

A third rather obvious question for our typology of the state is whether it is colonial (o) or not (p)—that is to say, whether the government of the country in question is basically dependent upon the government of another country quite clearly distinct. In this case church-state relations in the dependent country tend to depend less upon the political and religious character of the colonial society and a great deal upon that of the ruling country. Thus church-state relations in Portuguese Africa have been dominated by the fact that Portugal itself is nominally an almost purely Catholic country; again, as a result of the establishment of the Church of England in England, the Anglican communion obtained what has been described as a quasi-establishment—a position of exceptional influence—in many colonies where its numerical strength was quite limited. On the other hand, there were limits to this, thus British colonial policy if anything over-protected the already established position of Islam in places such as Northern Nigeria and coastal Tanganyika. But this remained essentially a decision of colonial policy and one which has in some ways been reversed since the coming of independence.

Fourthly, we can usefully distinguish between states which have major regional, cultural and tribal divisions within them (q) and those which have not (r), particularly if those divisions are tending towards open conflict and even the breakdown of state unity. Structurally, when a state successfully tackles a social situation of this kind, it is often through a federal arrangement, but all societies are not capable of receiving this. In situations of this sort church-state relations acquire an added complexity. A church may be identified by its membership with one division of society and consequently espouse its cause with enthusiasm, or it may feel that one section is seriously oppressed and it has a duty to speak out on its behalf, or it may judge that its own future security requires it to show some support for whichever party is likely to hold political power after the crisis. In situations of state crisis church-state relations, hitherto calm, also suddenly become tense: church leaders, like other people of influence, are drawn into taking sides and find themselves committing their people with them. Though, equally, in a national crisis churches may find themselves torn apart as much as the nation as a whole. In circumstances of this kind one church will come through almost unaffected, uninfluenced and perhaps uninfluencing: another will be deeply involved, even rent in two, both because of its membership pattern and the character of its leadership, and because of a sense of its task within situations of human conflict and oppression.

Secular and non-secular states, democratic and non-democratic, colonial and non-colonial, states struggling with a major rift in society and those not so faced—these four alternatives may not provide us with a fully adequate typology of the state for our purposes, but they do at least indicate the sort of qualities in a state which can affect the nature of church-state relations in a fairly basic way.

The structures of the state depend upon the structure of society, and the third area we need to consider is the typology of human societies. Both church and state reflect and are profoundly moulded by the basic shape of a human society derived from its kinship, economic and cultural characteristics. An authoritarian state is quite a different thing in a peasant, largely non-literate world and in an urban technological society, and its relations with the church will be quite different too. It is here that the African dimension most clearly takes over and can provide a decisively specific component within our over-all picture.

One could tentatively suggest a fairly simple typology of societies according to the following four alternatives in order to provide at least a springboard for an analysis of society as the determining ground beneath church-state relations.

i. On the one hand there are societies where religious belief and practice are a manifest and unquestioned part of ordinary life (s) and there are societies (t) in which there is a recognised divorce between the religious and the secular, even if they may on occasion be deliberately linked, and in which it is quite easy for people to opt out of religious life altogether without this greatly affecting other activities and relationships. The secularism of society is a deeper matter than the secularism of the state.

ii. We may contrast societies in which there is a clear chasm between a small elite and the vast mass of the people according to wealth, status or education **(u)** and societies in which the gap is very much less, in which basic rights are shared equally and a large middle class plays a major role **(v)**. The former group can be exemplified by medieval societies in western Europe, by pre-revolutionary Russia and—with a clearly different pattern—many African countries today; the latter is exemplified by most European countries in modern times.

iii. There is thirdly the difference between societies in which the decisive bonds and influences in most people's lives are on a small scale—village, kinship, the local market and shrine, the oral passing on of the learning of the elders **(w)**, and societies in which bonds tend to be on a large scale—town, the extended trading and industrial company, trade union, national educational system, TV network **(x)**.

iv. Finally, we can contrast societies whose shape and character (according to the categories of **i**, **ii**, **iii** and other criteria) are fairly stable **(y)**, and those in which massive and rapid social change is going on, including religious and ideological change **(z)**. Such change will be recreating the economy, basic mechanisms and cultural foundations of the society.

To generalise, it could be claimed that African societies tended in the past to fall into categories **s** and **w**, in this conforming to a 'medieval' European pattern, but they diverged from the latter in not fitting into category **u**. In so far as they are '**u**' societies today, this is largely a recent development, the result of 'Western' influences, economic, educational and political, which have created a new type of elite. Today they are also mostly in the **z** category; rapid social change is precisely breaking down the traditional character summarised by **s**, **w** and, in their own way, **v**.

As regards **(i)**, a notable paradox in present day Africa is that while the basic pattern of life does indeed remain that of **s**, yet the 'church'—or organised religion—is frequently Christian while the deeper religio-social unity is non-christian, and as a consequence the church instead of defending, drawing upon and institutionalising the ingrained religious practice of society, tends instead to clash with it. Consequently, in confrontation with the state, the Christian church or churches—even where they are theoretically the religion of the majority of the people—cannot easily fall back upon the support of the deeper religious instincts of the common man.

As regards **(ii)**, in **u** societies a church may either really straddle the social gap, or it may exist wholly within the submerged majority, or again—whatever its overall membership—be effectively controlled by the ruling elite.

As regards (iv), church-state tension is often a consequence of wider changes in the economic and educational structures of the whole of society: the church leadership may not understand what is happening and clings to a pattern of life and a way of participating in the organisation of the community which was accepted by all in the earlier society as suitable, but which is no longer viable or appears archaic within that which is now emerging.

It is in some of these basic areas of the shape of society that Africa today probably presents an over-all situation seriously different from almost anything to be found elsewhere; these factors control the surface both of state and church and, as we analyse apparently familiar patterns of church-state alliance or confrontation, we must continually bear in mind the type of society in which the representatives of both are operating.

Whatever the character of society, whatever the character of the state and whatever the character of the church, most churches find at least a modus vivendi with most states, most of the time. The character of each stimulates it to be either protective, co-operative, or downright suspicious towards its opposite number, as the case may be. But co-operation or conflict will in the end be related more to particular issues, to that area of shared interest, of overlap, which I have already pointed to, and it is in these issues that we find the precise grounds for establishment, persecution and the rest. It is, then, to an analysis of these particular issues that we should now turn. It is clear that in some ages and places the area of overlap has been very large indeed—almost every activity of the state seems to involve the church as well, and very many of the church's activities involve the state: the payment of tax includes the support of the church, church ministers are also state officials for certain purposes, state officials have regularly to attend church services, church leaders are necessarily included in the government, and so forth. In other circumstances the area of overlap is very small and may indeed be little more than the basic reality that members of the one society are also members of the other and that in some sides of life the regulations of the two societies touch upon the same matters, confirming or contradicting one another.

Overlap, however, there always is; and it may well be far more extensive than is at first apparent. Which are its chief elements and the things which make either for active co-operation or conscious tension? Let us consider the reasons for co-operation first by putting the simple question: Where can the state profit?

First, the support of a church can provide it with an added sacral dimension, increasing its authority and strengthening its claim to loyalty. The king is anointed by the Church as God's chosen one; civil disobedience is sinful. It will bring about not only man's punishment, but God's. If one dies for one's country, one can be sure that one is doing the will of God. Particularly in times of stress this can be a considerable contribution that the church is making to the state so long as people admit the authority of the church to say such things. If the leaders of the state in fact themselves believe in God, this dimension may go further; it not only strengthens the loyalty of their people, but helps to ensure that they are right with God. Earthly success may depend upon prayer; the state cannot afford to neglect the spiritual dimension and therefore needs people to pray on its behalf—particularly as its enemies may also be praying hard.

Secondly, at a social-cultural level the Church has considerable influence through its services, its preaching, its literature and its own educational institutions. If the state has, for instance, a language policy—wishing to encourage the use of one language, discourage that of another—the good will of the Church in this can be of the greatest importance, particularly in societies where a large part of cultural life has in fact a religious aspect. Other sides of policy too, both with regard to home and foreign affairs, can be assisted if some encouragement be given from the pulpit whether it be a matter of volunteering for the army or digging canals or participating in a literacy campaign; there are certainly modern African governments as there have for centuries been European governments which expect such help to be given from time to time.

Thirdly, the church frequently shoulders various secular services for which the state sees some need but which it has not the inclination, perhaps the means or the personnel, to maintain directly—schools, hospitals, orphanages. The church considers the running of these to be proper and important areas for its own mission, rendering service to those in need and establishing a forum for the teaching of its doctrine. In some countries these have not been regarded as matter for state concern, at least in any systematic way, in others they are now regarded as almost wholly the function of the state; but in many countries a sharing of responsibility has been felt to be the most fitting approach, the state leaving much of the work to other agencies while providing some assistance, financial and otherwise, including overall supervision.

It is clear that by responding to the state's needs in these various areas, the Church too may be gaining considerable advantages: fields of work and influence, financial and legal support, possibly a favoured position from the viewpoint of the dissemination of ideas. The closer one's own links with the state, the less opportunity will there be for rival religious bodies and ideologies.

With these fields of co-operation in mind, we can more easily trace the other side of the picture—the reasons for tension between church and state. Here I would suggest six chief areas.

1. Close co-operation leads to an ever greater measure of state control over the Church. Its secular responsibilities may have become so important that the state is loth to leave the church to appoint its own leaders, decide its own policies, or speak its mind freely lest this involve disagreement with the government. Co-operation becomes servitude, and while this may be acceptable to some segments of the church, there are other elements which judge that its essential mission and freedom have been lost through privilege and therefore attack the state and the church's connection with the state in order to re-establish the church's proper autonomy.

2. Close co-operation can well lead in the opposite direction to an over large measure of church control over important sides of national life, particularly if the state has been rather weak. The church has become almost a state within a state, running the country's educational system, paying thousands of laymen, monopolising senior posts for the clergy and so forth. The consequence is a growth of resentment against the church, anti-clericalism, and a state policy to exclude the church from influence in 'secular' life.

3. The closer forms of church-state collaboration, roughly summarised by the word 'establishment', imply a relationship between the state and a single church; but there may be other churches in the country, and the consequence of such an arrangement with one church is tension with the others or even their persecution. Here, either the state is being used by the church to victimise or suppress its rivals in a religious or ecclesiastical conflict, or the deeper initiative really comes from the state itself, deriving from a political decision that religious uniformity is desirable for the strengthening of unity within the nation.

4. The church may consider certain laws or behaviour of the state as immoral and either forbid its own members to conform or further issue a public condemnation. This cause of conflict may be regarded indeed as the most basic one, deriving from the nature of the church as such: a religious-moral society claiming God's authority to witness to what is right and wrong. It does not follow as the first three from a situation of prior church-state co-operation. Cases of this are of course legion: alleged government oppression of a race, region or class, or indeed the unjust treatment of an individual; compulsory military service; compulsory vaccination; legal abortion; exclusion of religious teaching from compulsory state schools....

The other side of this is a church's refusal to participate in activities which the state considers to be not immoral at all but very necessary—emperor worship, saluting the flag.... The precise cause of conflict and of the church's persecution becomes not the church's protest but the civil disobedience of its members.

5. A church may be very closely linked by its membership with a certain group in society, probably an under-privileged one. It may indeed have arisen precisely as the spiritual expression of the latter's protest against its conditions. The church can then become closely identified with the political struggle of a certain class or region for local independence, autonomy, advancement, a fair deal. In this situation the church may have almost become unofficially 'established' within a sub-group of the country, whose interests are seen as opposed to those of the centre, and it is using its influence precisely against the cultural and political policy of the established government.

6. Finally, church-state tension may be caused by the external international connections of the church. Links with a hostile foreign power (where its co-religionists are a majority) can add to its difficulties within a country (where it is a minority) and even bring about its proscription—as, for example when Roman Catholics in Elizabethan England were thought to be in league with Spain. Christians in seventeenth-century Japan and in late nineteenth-century China, Roman Catholics in Ethiopia in several epochs have all been judged anti-national and treated accordingly because of the links of their churches with enemy powers.

We are now provided, I believe, with a basic typology of church-state relations. In the distant past these relations had often a certain simplicity in that there was only one church in a particular country, or at least one main church and one or two dissident groups. In the modern situation this has generally been far from the case, although the old pattern still largely holds in such countries as Spain and Portugal. But the normal modern situation is one of a considerable number of churches and an analysis of church-state relations in a given situation has to bear in mind the different condition, past history and present character of a number of churches. It may happen that the state's relations with the churches within its country are noticeably diverse— friendly with some, opposed to others almost oblivious of a third group (e.g. in some modern African countries, friendly with the main line mission churches, hostile to Watchtower, oblivious of some smaller independent churches). In the recent past the relations of a state with Catholics and Protestants were often clearly different; this would be encouraged by the churches themselves because of their intrinsic opposition to one another. However, the very multiplicity of churches is contributing to a new unicity. One recognisable characteristic of the ecclesiastical scene in our time is for the churches themselves to come increasingly together—for the dimensions of ecumenicity to grow, that of exclusivity to decrease. If there is relatively seldom an organic union, there is a new pattern of quite intimate consultation and co-operation. Consequently viz à viz the state a new church unity is in many places appearing, manifested by, for instance, the growth of national councils of churches. This development is to some extent matched by increasingly obvious differences of attitude within a single church.

The study of modern church-state relations has then to bear in mind all the time not only the changes which are going on at this time in the whole pattern of society, but also that the churches themselves are changing. In fact during the last fifteen years some churches have witnessed an almost revolutionary change of attitudes as regards the priorities of church concern, at least among the younger clergy, and this may add to the bewilderment of the detached observer of the scene. Representatives of a church which a few years ago struggled with grim determination to exclude heretics or extend its own schools system, may today blithely share its buildings with those same heretics and argue that the control of an extensive school system is a crippling burden for the church which should be shouldered by the state precisely so as to leave the church free to get on with its own true work.

An adequate typology of church-state relations has to accept the immense diversity in the self-understanding churches have of themselves, as equally in the concerns and structures of government. Church and state have argued over the centuries over almost every possible thing; they have also worked together in an extraordinary variety of ways. At times they have simply attempted to ignore one another. We have examples from Africa over the last decade to illustrate many of the classical patterns. Small intransigent churches like the Lumpa in Zambia or the Witnesses in Malawi come into open conflict with the state and are pro-scribed; middle range churches in many countries co-operate with the state, at times with enthusiasm, at others with a certain reserve; large scale majority type churches identify with the state in Ethiopia or Portuguese Africa or are drawn into a power struggle in Zaire where church meetings have been banned and the cardinal archbishop was forced into temporary exile. In situations of civil war a strong minority church may largely identify itself, as did the Catholic Church in eastern Nigeria, with a region in revolt. One could continue almost indefinitely ringing the changes.

A typology is a tool of work with a necessarily rough edge and a pragmatic, half abitrary, character to it. It helps us to sort out the infinite diversity within the human condition, asserting parallels here, contrasts there in a systematic and coherent way, throwing light upon a particular situation by establishing it within a wide framework of reference which will, nonetheless, never finally reduce recognition of its historic individuality. At the same time it deepens our understanding of the universal condition, in this case the perennial relationship between relig-ious institution and political institution which reflects the ap-parently irrepressible human need for a duality of final reference in social structure.

For all of us who in one way or another dwell within the frontier land of church and state, whether it be in England or the United States, Italy or Ireland, Zaire or South Korea, a some-what detached analysis—as mine has attempted to be—of a whole range of variables which can result in many thousands of different combinations may still serve a practical and necessary purpose: a sound appreciation of just where we stand here and now.

6

Mission and unity. From Edinburgh via Uppsala to Nairobi

Professor Latourette, a veteran ecumenist and missiologist whose many-volumed *History of the Expansion of Christianity* is a standard work, remarked that 'it cannot be said too often or too emphatically that the ecumenical movement arose from the missionary movement and continues to have at its heart world-wide evangelism'.[1] In ecumenical circles this has been a truism for a great many years: everywhere in the world Christian division reduces the credibility of the Church and reunion must bring with it a great step forward in evangelism. 'Christian mission,' says Mgr Francis Davis, 'is hampered by lack of unity; and disunity is cited as at least one cause of the continued decline in the influence and numerical strength of the Churches of this country.'[2] During the sixty years of the organized ecumenical movement, from 1910 down to the present moment, this intrinsic and decisive link between mission and unity has been asserted times beyond number. The Edinburgh Missionary Conference of that year was at once the great start to the ecumenical movement of the century and in John R. Mott's words 'the most creative event of modern world missions'.[3]

If such statements are examined, they will be seen to be asserting a number of different though related points:
1. Theologically mission and unity are inseparable: 'May they all be one that the world may believe.'
2. As a matter of fact the urge to help end Christian divisions has arisen most strongly in this century among missionary workers.
3. The division of Christian communions adds a very serious and unnecessary problem for the non-Christian approaching the Gospel.

[1]Rouse and Neill, *A History of the Ecumenical Movement*, p. 362.
[2]*New Blackfriars*, January 1969, pp. 211-12.
[3]*Addresses and Papers of John R. Mott*, V, p. xvii.

4. The division of Christian communions detracts from the credibility of Christianity in the minds of Christians, especially young Christians. It prevents effective witness and is a chief cause of the decline of the Church.

5. Where unity is achieved, there will be and is a great increase in the vitality, membership and sense of mission of the Church.

Many ecumenical workers would, I think, take it for granted that all these statements are indubitably true. Nor is my purpose here by any means to challenge them in their entirety. The sad consequences of division and hostility in missionary activity, and even of the large scale turning of that activity to the 'conversion' of members of other Churches, have been only too obvious. Nevertheless there is today a growing doubt on one point or another, and it is at least evident that much which has been asserted about the mission-unity relationship in the past is uncritical, greatly over-simplified and perhaps even untrue. Indeed when one considers the vast missionary work of the last hundred and fifty years carried on in division and the way, on human standards of judgement, God has greatly blessed it, it could seem one-sided to the point of blindness to speak of 'the disaster of mission without unity'.[4]

In attempting to explore the question, I will be working far more from Protestant experience than from Catholic, just because nearly all the movements and tendencies involved began earlier in the Protestant communions than the Catholic. This is not only true of ecumenism, but also of the logical development within the missionary movement. Hence we can, I believe, helpfully interpret what is happening within the Catholic missionary movement today by considering what has already happened in the Protestant world since the International Missionary Council's meeting at Tambaram in 1938. Nevertheless we are increasingly one community participating in a common world. Our experiences and future tasks are to be interpreted jointly, not apart.

It is useful to begin by listing a number of phenomena. Firstly, there is the fact that in the half century following 1910 while ecumenical enthusiasm among the chief non-Catholic Western Churches has steadily increased, their evangelistic missionary commitment—at least 'overseas'—has almost equally steadily declined. Both developments have been most marked in the second half of the period. At the same time the evangelistic

[4] V. Hayward, 'Prospects for Ecumenical Unity in Mission', *One in Christ*, 1970, 1, p. 17.

activity of Protestant Churches with a small ecumenical commitment, or none at all, has greatly increased. As a result today the majority of overseas Protestant missionaries represent the smaller, often very fundamentalist communions unconnected with the World Council of Churches. In the Roman Catholic Church in the fifty years following 1910 ecumenism was frowned upon and the number of missionaries overseas steadily increased. Since 1960, however, a wave of ecumenism has transformed the Catholic Church, at the same time vocations to missionary societies have drastically fallen—above all in those countries, such as Holland, most deeply affected by new ecumenical attitudes. It is in those countries, notably Italy, where ecumenism has so far spread least, that the decrease in missionary vocations is also least apparent. It is certain that there are other major factors involved in this decrease in willingness to accept a fulltime missionary commitment, but it would be rash to deny that the spread of ecumenism may have something to do with it.

Next, the great advance in evangelism hoped for as a result of reunion schemes has not in fact happened. This has been pointed out in the case of the Church of South India by its own frank report *Renewal and Advance*, which could even go so far as to say: 'It can hardly be doubted that the increased introversion of the Church, which has a bearing on many evils, has to a considerable extent been the result of union.'[5] It is quite evident to me in the case of the United Church of Zambia, and it could probably be easily documented in other places as well. It is in the case of British Methodism a central thesis of Robert Currie's *Methodism Divided: a study in the Sociology of Ecumenicalism.*[6] In anticipation of the Methodist merger in Britain of 1932 the *Methodist Recorder* asserted in 1929 that 'with the consummation of union a great forward movement on quite unprecedented lines is anticipated; is indeed inevitable'.[7] Statistics, however, reveal a steady decrease in membership in the following thirty-two years of 140,000.

It can be shown sociologically that unity schemes are in fact often most favourably received in Churches which are declining rather than vigorously missionary. In the words of another critical sociologist 'amalgamation and alliance occur when institutions are weak rather than when they are strong'.[8] Or to

[5] M. Gibbard, *Unity is not Enough*, Mowbray, 1965 pp. 75-6. 103-4.
[6] Faber and Faber, 1968.
[7] Currie, p. 299.
[8] Bryan Wilson, *Religion in Secular Society*, Watts, 1966, p. 142.

quote Currie, 'a denomination with a falling membership to population ratio, reduced turnover, ageing membership and dwindling frontal growth is ready for the lateral growth opportunities available in the ecumenical option'.[9] Not only in Britain but also in the young Churches it is often noticeable that it is the relatively static groups which are most interested in systematic ecumenism. The strongly missionary ones are really too busy growing and evangelizing to bother. In the words of another sociologist who has made his research in Africa, 'Sects proliferate where people are enthusiastic about religion and reunion is often a token of decline'.[10]

The arrival of the White Fathers in Buganda in 1879 exactly in the place where the Church Missionary Society had arrived a little time before and the consequent bitter rivalry between the two missions, has often been lambasted by Protestant writers as a missionary disaster. Objectively it would be difficult to substantiate this. Nowhere in Africa was there such a rapid and serious turning to Christianity as in Buganda in the following twenty-five years. Bitter denominational rivalry, regrettable as one may hold it to have been on all sorts of grounds, seemed to act as a first-class spur for evangelistic work. Indeed in general throughout the missionary field it must often be admitted that the fear of another denomination getting in first has been a continual incitement to lasting missionary efforts.

This point becomes even more true when the Christian attitude to other religions is considered. A great part of missionary motivation has been derived from a conviction of the absolutely overwhelming importance of being a Christian and not a 'heathen' (Moslem, Buddhist, Animist, etc.). The fact that in ecumenical circles today there is also a strong stress upon the positive values in other world religions, and even on the priority of dialogue to evangelization, upon in fact the existence of a 'wider oecumene' makes many people reluctant to commit themselves to explicitly evangelistic tasks. It was a matter of prime importance in the past to many people in England or Scotland that Africans became Protestants and not Catholics, but still more that they became Christians and not Moslems.[11] This type of concern is hardly compatible with a wider ecumenism stressing the virtues of

[9]Op. cit., p. 110.
[10]J. D. Y. Peel, African Digest, February 1968, p. 24.
[11]The following sentence, almost too obvious in the atmosphere of Edinburgh, would have been nearly inconceivable in that of Uppsala: 'In Malaya Christian missions must strain every nerve to prevent Islam from gaining the heathen tribes, and win them for Christ' (Mott, op. cit., p. 35).

dialogue. It is not difficult to understand why the number of missionaries decreases as the current ecumenical attitude in its totality spreads. In the Protestant Churches, where, of course, this process has gone on for far longer than among Catholics, the reaction or backlash to it is now also very strong. Conservative evangelicals[12] will complain that ecumenists have sold the missionary pass, a betrayal seen by many to culminate in Uppsala 1968. Two years later, 1970, a group of German theologians published the uncompromising *Frankfurt Declaration* condemning the 'insidious falsification' now going on in missionary and ecumenical circles, whereby dialogue with the religions and 'revolutionary involvement' are seen as 'contemporary forms of Christian mission'. Even so moderate and ecumenically committed an evangelical as Canon Douglas Webster can say: 'I would hazard a guess that the time will come—perhaps soon—when those with the most knowledge and experience of real mission will consider the Uppsala report on mission to be little short of a sell-out to the diseased and confused spirit of our age.'[13] Back in 1954 Professor Latourette remarked that 'an increasing proportion of the missionaries from the "older Churches" are from bodies which do not join in the many co-operative enterprises or in the ecumenical movement'.[14] This has become more and more true. Lesslie Newbigin, a particularly distinguished missionary ecumenist and the first director of the World Council of Churches' Division of World Mission and Evangelism, has recently discussed the conservative evangelical conviction that the Protestant ecumenical movement has got its priorities disastrously wrong: 'The fruit of these convictions has been seen in the growth of missionary organizations apart from the major Churches which together recruit and support a larger number

[12]The term 'conservative evangelical' is, like most religious descriptions, unsatisfactory but cannot be avoided. It refers both to some Protestant Churches, mostly with a particularly fundamentalist character, that have not joined the WCC and to many, more Reformation-minded, members of Churches that have joined. Naturally they do not all think the same way; moreover much of the thinking characteristic of the WCC has come from men connected with missionary societies whose inspiration in the past has been 'evangelical'. Certainly conservative evangelicals within the Church of England, as represented for instance by the National Evangelical Anglican Congress at Keele in April 1967, have come to a far more positive approach both to the ecumenical movement and to concern for 'the problems of our society' than is characteristic of the movement as a whole in world terms; but then they also provide fewer overseas missionaries.

[13]*Bible and Mission* (British and Foreign Bible Society), p. 3.

[14]*The Christian World Mission in our Day*, Harper and Brothers, 1954, p. 154.

of foreign missionaries than do all the agencies related to the World Council of Churches put together.'[15] Newbigin is referring not only to Pentecostals and to the groups led by Carl McIntyre but to such bodies as the Overseas Missionary Fellowship, the Southern Baptist Convention, the Christian and Missionary Alliance and others.[16] To them can be added considerable groups within Churches related to the WCC that are distrustful of its current policies. Of such, evidently, Canon Webster is an example. To return to Newbigin: 'Missionary thinking in ecumenical circles has moved during the past fifteen years away from the kind of concern which could lead to a meeting with Conservative Evangelicals' (*ibid*). Hence today, far from it being self-evident that the call to mission is a call to unity, Newbigin can sadly remark that 'these two words no longer seem to belong together. They pull in opposite directions' (p. 257). Without taking nearly so pessimistic a view of the Uppsala report as does Webster, it would still seem to be only too obvious that despite Professor Latourette the ecumenical movement has not effectively at its heart today 'world-wide evangelism'.

Clearly there are in this divorce, if such it is, a number of separate phenomena. Firstly, there is the theological revolution of this century whereby many Christians in different communions have come to realize that Christian witness has got to take account of **(a)** how in one way or another the interpretation of the Bible and of all subsequent doctrinal statements has to be done across an understanding of the culturally conditioning factors of other ages built into those documents and only relatively significant for our age; **(b)** the inclusiveness of the love of God: that is indeed a biblical theme but it has frequently been swallowed up by a church exclusiveness. A realization of the open possibility of 'salvation' outside the visible Church and for those who have never heard the name of Christ so much as mentioned, as of the positive way in which God's grace is offered to all men and necessarily through their own religious and cultural values, is bound to undermine some motives of mission and equally bound to generate a sense of near betrayal in mission-minded people who are still predominantly moved by those very incentives; **(c)** the relationship of explicit witness to other forms of service

[15]'Call to Mission—A Call to Unity?' in *The Church Crossing Frontiers*, 1969, pp. 254-5.
[16]Stephen Neill asserts that while more than a third of nominal Christians in the world belong to Churches included in the WCC, barely one-sixth of the missionary work in the world is being done by Churches which adhere to the Council (*A History of Christian Mission*, Penguin, 1964, p. 460).

and of both to the here-and-now human condition of those one has in mind to reach. Failure to do this has helped to render ineffectual so very much missionary work in the past. 'Mission' in fact is a necessary amalgam of 'evangelism' and secular service. To identify it almost purely with the first is to falsify its true character; (d) the dechristianized character of old Christian countries. In the past concern with foreign mission often went with a vast blindness to the pressing internal missionary needs of 'sending' countries such as Britain and France.

The disengagement of ecumenism and the missionary movement has been a fair time developing. It seems to be the case that a great deal of vigour slowly passed out of the old style missionary commitment of the major Protestant Churches during the middle years of this century. Perhaps their most effective period lay before and after the great international meeting at Edinburgh in 1910 and on to the further meeting at Jerusalem in 1928. Subsequently one can sense a decline, partly effected by the slump and then the war, partly by a questioning of purposes and an alteration in the priority of concerns. It was related also to a realization—manifested at Tambaram in 1938—that one of the great ends had somehow been achieved: self-reliant local Churches really were emerging and one consequence of this was a less sure sense on the part of the 'sending' Churches of what they were now meant to do, while at home the need for new forms of 'industrial mission' and such like could be a lot clearer.

At Edinburgh in 1910 there was no problem as to what the Gospel was nor the absolute duty of the Christian world to propagate it nor the extreme suitability of the present time for that work of propagation. 'The evangelization of the world in this generation' was a clear, possible and obligatory programme. That famous watchword had already been widely used in the international Student Christian Movement but it came to sum up the spirit of Edinburgh and to be the keynote of the coming years. But as these passed, problems steadily mounted. The complexity of the missionary task was more sensitively understood by many of those most committed to it—but by no means by all. J. H. Oldham, secretary of the Edinburgh Conference, secretary of the continuation committee, secretary of the International Missionary Council from its formation, was probably the man most instrumental in bringing this about.[17] He was the principal organizer

[17]For a first general study of the man and his work see J. W. C. Dougall in the *International Review of Mission*, January 1970, pp. 8-22.

of Jerusalem, 1928, the first great international missionary gathering since Edinburgh, in which a whole new emphasis came to the fore, but so also as a consequence an increasing split in missionary ranks. Jerusalem's particular character as a meeting derives from its awareness of the social implications of Gospel and mission. The Council prefaced its official statement by affirming 'with all the power at its command' that 'the Gospel of Christ contains a message, not only for the individual soul, but for the world of social organization and economic relations in which individuals live'. William Hogg, the historian of the International Missionary Council, comments: 'Hitherto the missionary objective had been thought of primarily in terms of geographic expansion, but Jerusalem pointed to large areas of life that must be brought effectively under the sway of Christian principle. That the Gospel is meant for individuals only and that its spread can be measured by tabulating the land areas where such individuals live it rejected as false assumptions. It insisted rather that every segment of human interest and activity must be won for Christ, that Christ is Lord over all life. In this Jerusalem extended the dimensions of traditional missionary thinking.'[18] But for many this extension of dimension was an illicit one. Jerusalem perhaps symbolizes that parting of the ways in modern Protestantism which has had so decisive an effect upon the strategy of mission. While Edinburgh's rather simple concept of evangelism received general praise, Jerusalem's social concern at once brought division. Dr Torm of Copenhagen University read a paper at the Continental Missions Conference in 1930 denouncing Jerusalem's 'Christian sociology'.[19] The German missionary movement as a whole was extremely strong on a 'pure Gospel' only being proclaimed, that is to say one 'without social implications'.[20] There could be, of

[18]W. R. Hogg, *Ecumenical Foundations: a History of the International Missionary Council and its Nineteenth-Century Background*, Harper and Brothers, 1952, pp. 250-1.

[19]Hogg, *op. cit.*, p. 252.

[20]See K. M. Beckmann, 'German Churches and Missions Face the Race Question', *International Review of Mission*, July 1970, pp. 311-15. One can see the division extremely clearly within the general missionary movement by comparing J. H. Oldham's speech at the 1926 Le Zoute missionary conference (pp. 162-70 of Edwin W. Smith, *The Christian Mission in Africa*, A Study based on the Proceedings of the International Conference at Le Zoute, Belgium, 1926) and Roland Allen's criticism of it *Le Zoute, A Critical Review of 'The Christian Mission in Africa'*, World Dominion Press, 1927. At the time Oldham was far more influential than Allen in missionary circles, but not so today, when Oldham's point of view remains dominant with one wing but a revival of Allen's outlook with another—the McGavran school.

course, the same reaction to the Life and Work Movement, developing at the same time. The Finnish Archbishop Johansson refused to attend the conference in Stockholm in 1925, because 'social, economic and political problems do not belong to the domain of the Church'. [21] These divisions of the 1920s seem to me significant for the whole subsequent course of events in the ecumenical and missionary movements.

The career of Jo Oldham is indicative of what happened to the Protestant missionary impetus. He and the American John R. Mott were the two oustanding figures in the international missionary movement after Edinburgh. In the words of W. H. Hogg, Oldham was 'the man whose mind more than that of any other person had shaped the International Missionary Council'.[22] Against the advice of Mott, Oldham accepted the chairmanship of the research commission of 'Life and Work' in preparation for the 1937 Oxford Conference on 'Church, Community and State', at which the formation of the World Council of Churches was in fact decided upon. More and more Oldham felt that mission could not be interpreted except across the tackling of such central problems as that title indicated. To understand how the secretary of the Edinburgh Conference understood 'the mission of the Church' a quarter of a century later one cannot do better than turn to the introductory volume of the Oxford papers entitled *The Church and its Function in Society* and written by Visser 't Hooft and Oldham. Next year at Tambaram Oldham's resignation as a secretary of the IMC was regretfully accepted. His sense of the width of mission passed via 'Life and Work' into the WCC. The true line of ecumenical succession runs Oldham, Visser 't Hooft, Philip Potter. In many ways it seems to me that Oldham was the father of Uppsala's concept of mission while Mott would rather have sympathized with its more conservative evangelical critics: 'The evangelization of the world in this generation' remained Mott's watchword for life, but in his use of it he was somehow increasingly isolated. In subsequent years it has, as a matter of fact, become more and more a missionary rallying cry for some groups of conservative evangelicals.[23]

In the post second war period the IMC appears to have lost much of its old imaginative clarity of purpose. Its meetings at Willingen in 1952 and Ghana in 1958 'seemed strangely unable to

[21]Bengt Sundkler. *Nathan Söderblom: His Life and Work*, Lutterworth, 1968, p. 359.

[22]*Op. Cit.*, p. 320.

[23]See H. Hans Hoekendijk, 'Evangelisation of the World in this Generation', *International Review of Mission*, January 1970, pp. 23-31.

give anything like a clear or strong lead ... somehow the direction was lost'.[24] The merging of the IMC with the WCC during the latter's third world assembly at New Delhi in 1961 was right and inevitable. Yet, it seems it was in some sense the merging of a rump whose decisive influence had greatly declined within the total world of Protestant mission: ecumenical creativity had already passed to the WCC whose own sense of mission, grounded in the tradition of 'Life and Work', had steadily deepened since its foundation at Amsterdam,[25] while as for numbers the majority of Protestant missionaries were no longer associated with the IMC. The choice seemed now clear: either adherence to the trend of modern theology, the co-operation of the major churches, a sophisticated care for the whole man but a weakened sense of urgency to proclaim an explicit Gospel, or a refusal to bend before the complexities of the modern world, but to announce instead a verbally-unchanging Gospel, countering the greater part of the ecumenical experience of a generation.

The divide became still clearer during the 1960s. Norman Goodall, the editor of the Uppsala report, has described the character of the Uppsala Assembly as follows: 'The most obvious and widely-acknowledged feature of the Assembly was its pre-occupation—at times, almost, its obsession—with the revolutionary ferment of our time, with questions of social and international responsibility, of war and peace and economic justice, with the pressing, agonizing physical needs of men, with the plight of the underprivileged, the homeless and starving, and with the most radical contemporary rebellions against all "establishments", civil and religious.'[26] The conservative evangelical response to this kind of thing—as also the conservative Catholic—is one of open alarm. Cardinal Willebrands, referring to a WCC conference at Zagorsk, remarked that 'it emerged clearly once again that it is easier to reach agreement on social problems than on points of faith. Christians and Christian Churches have always been able to talk and act together in society in spite of their differences of conviction in matters of faith and church order.'[27] One knows what Willebrands is referring to, nevertheless the

[24]Erik W. Nielsen, 'The Role of the IMC' in *The Ghana Assembly of the IMC, 1958*, ed. Ronald Orchard, p. 188. The whole essay is of great interest.

[25]See, for instance, R. Jasper's life of George Bell, especially chapter 16. Bell was the first chairman of the central committee; also Norman Goodall, 'Evanston and the World Mission of the Church', *International Review of Mission*, 1955, pp. 85-92.

[26]*The Uppsala Report*, 1968, WCC, Geneva, p. xvii

[27]'Common Witness and Proselytism'. *One in Christ*, 1970. p. 8.

statement seems seriously misleading. Christians may not indeed divide on social problems in a denominational way, but they do still—indeed increasingly—divide. As we have seen, at the very heart of the conservative evangelical criticism of the way mission has developed in ecumenical circles ever since Jerusalem, 1928, has been that of too much concern with 'social problems'. That the critics are simply not represented at many ecumenical conferences does not mean that they do not exist. It means that they have opted out of the movement. For the WCC ecumenists the mission of the Church today, for which unity is needed, has as an integral part such things as the struggle against racialism. The Division of World Mission and Evangelism is particularly involved in the WCC's current 'Programme for Combatting Racism'. Here above all current WCC ecumenism is the heir of Oldham, whose important book *Christianity and the Race Problem* was published as long ago as 1924, and it was Oldham who got the Jerusalem Conference to give special attention to the issue of 'Mission and Race Conflict'.[28] All this is behind the WCC's current support of anti-racialist organizations, even such bodies as use violent means and are illegal in their own countries. For their critics this is a straight betrayal of the purity of the Gospel and of mission. For the one, to preach the Gospel has nothing to do with a political concern of any kind, for the other, to opt out of politics and the political dimensions of service, development work and the righting of injustice, is itself a betrayal of the Gospel and of authentic mission.

The issue of the grants to liberation movements has indeed become a *cause célèbre* in which the World Council has been grossly misrepresented time and again. Nobody would protest about the wickedness of a church giving money for some medical or educational purpose to a government, even an oppressive or unpopular government. Yet when the churches gave such grants to Frelimo and PAIGC all hell was let loose not only by politicians on the other side who had always regarded the churches as docile instruments for subjugating the poor, but also by ecclesiastics, particularly ecclesiastics within England's established church. Perhaps a few of them may have had second thoughts now that some of the movements in question have actually taken over the government of their countries! Few symbols reveal men's central commitments better than the gift and reception of money. The vast financial interchange between the churches and colonial governments did not apparently disturb the consciences

[28]See the *International Review of Mission*, July 1970, editorial and elsewhere.

78

of these gentlemen, but the infinitely smaller grants of the World Council to groups of Africans struggling desperately to be free against a system of quite monstrous oppression did so.

This is but one indication of the truth that religious conservatives who advocate the necessity of a 'pure Gospel' are very seldom themselves detached politically. Not to challenge the establishment is to accept and strengthen it. The missionary who preached a very 'pure Gospel' was the natural supporter of colonialism. The mutual support of Billy Graham and President Nixon in the United States, conservative Catholic encouragement in Britain (including leaders of the *Pro Fide* movement) for the selling of arms to the South African government, are instances of a rival political stance taken up by those who reject a theological assessment of the radical political implications of the Gospel mission. At this level, faced with the pressures of today's world and the sense of urgent personal commitment to respond to them, any sort of reconciliation between the two attitudes seems extremely unlikely. And it is very difficult indeed to remain neutral.

The same decade that has brought these questions to the fore has posed in an equally challenging way a reconsideration of the central content of the explicit Gospel—the essential of the *kerygma*. What is the Gospel message? Here, certainly, the WCC has not taken up a position in the same way; yet in general the theological circles of the 1960s, both Protestant and Catholic, which have been most ecumenically involved, include many people, especially of the younger generation, deeply affected by the work of Bultmann, of the 'death of God' theology, and in general by the winds of secularization. Perhaps the effect of a post-Bultmannian approach is the most serious from our viewpoint. What are the central doctrines of the missionary Church? The ascension, miracles, the virgin birth, the bodily resurrection, every individual word of Jesus is questioned as to its authenticity and reinterpreted symbolically. Finally little is left of the particularity of the Incarnation and the unique significance of Christ. The old missionary calling simply fades away if there is no clear message, at once true and obviously of overwhelming importance both for the scholarly bearer and the simple hearer (or, for that matter, the simple bearer and the scholarly hearer). The effect of this can be as obvious today in a Catholic as in a Protestant seminary. The conservative evangelical (and Catholic) is as aghast with a questioning of the bodily resurrection as of involvement in the revolutionary arena.

Has the missionary Church today, then, no alternative between a literary fundamentalism on the one hand and a demythologized proclamation that 'the business of Jesus goes on' upon the other?

The gap between some radical ecumenically-orientated circles and some missionary-minded circles reveals itself as a chasm between two main types of theology in the Christian world today. As has already been remarked, this is not chiefly a division between Churches, it is a division within Churches. Moreover it is often true that in Churches closely linked with the WCC a majority of the clergy, or at least the more vocal clergy, may hold strongly to one type of theology, while a larger majority of the laity may hold to the other. Of course, many people would refuse to commit themselves fully to either side, but the sense of the tension is very clear. For one side or the other need not be wholly right. If one side appears trapped in non-historical conceptions of the Word of God and of Christian doctrine, the other may have been carried too far by the uncertainties of post-Bultmannian exegesis and by the transient enthusiasms of today's secular world and its current fixation with revolution into obscuring the ultimately primal necessity for mission to offer explicit witness to God's revelation in Jesus Christ.

Further, the division is not only theological but structural: altered concepts of mission inevitably require new structures, but while the concepts do not fully gel, the new structures are naturally not forthcoming. The division here is certainly not an absolute one, nevertheless it is becoming increasingly clear between those who are basically satisfied with nineteenth-century structures for mission and those who are convinced that such structures and the image that has gone with them are becoming more and more inappropriate in today's world; that while they may partly satisfy the people within them and who support them, they are no longer an effective implement in today's society—especially in the third world—and that much about them can even be a disservice to the cause of effective mission.

With structures goes the whole issue of missionary numbers. Does the present age call for as many full-time missionaries as possible? To one side, even to ask the question is a betrayal. Time and again we still hear Roman Catholic and Conservative Evangelical appeals for more full time, old type missionaries. The expansion in missionary numbers was doubtless providential for the first part of the twentieth century. Today the situation is quite different and, in the opinion of many of us, a large number of western missionaries in Afro-Asia may actually be a disservice if it hinders the development of a truly indigenous witness, and enhances a neo-colonialist image. Hence, while Edinburgh's *leitmotif* was that there was 'an opening of doors in all parts of the world' and a consequent 'vast enlargement in the number of qualified workers' needed,[29] Professor Freytag in the most significant paper read at the 1958 IMC meeting in Ghana could so dwell instead on the theme of 'limitation' as practically to produce an appeal for 'fewer and fewer missionaries'. 'Who would want to impede the development of Churches which in some degree depends on the absence of missionaries?'[30] In the words of Erik Nielsen, commenting on that meeting: 'It is a strange line which leads from Edinburgh to Ghana.'[31] In essentials I am personally convinced that it was a strategically correct one. In the Catholic Church the moral of Freytag is only now being attended to. And that by very few people. The Catholic response to a sharp decline in missionary vocations is still, too often, a purely defensive and negative one. As Victor Hayward points out: the possibility is hardly envisaged that God 'no longer needs as many missionary priests'.[32] If Holland and France have dried up, let us look instead for more men in Malta, Poland or Mexico. The conservative evangelical view is here quite the same. One of the strongest criticisms that can be made of this position is that it has profoundly failed to realize the missionary implications of the change both of world climate and of the state of the younger Churches in the sixty years since Edinburgh. Even accepting the old-fashioned scope of mission almost unchanged, the old-fashioned means are today increasingly counter-productive and the rather slight effect of much more recently initiated mission work undertaken on the old patterns is evidence of this.

How do you count 'missionaries' anyhow? While those with the traditional approach will count as missionaries only those sponsored by recognized missionary societies and paid out of church funds, those with the new approach often prefer to commit themselves to mission within a fully secular context. It is impossible to enumerate people who approach mission in this latter way, hence figures of a decline in the number of 'missionaries' in ecumenical circles by the very nature of the case only tell half the story. The whole comparison, in fact, is

[29] John R. Mott, *Addresses and Papers*, V, pp. 23 and 34.
[30] 'Changes in the Patterns of Western Missions', in R. Orchard, *op. cit.*, p. 140.
[31] *Op. cit.*, p. 201.
[32] *Op. cit.*, *One in Christ*, 1970, p. 21.

presupposing the one point of view in attempting a comparison between the two. It is also true that the acceptability of missionaries in large numbers is related to their colour and nationality. The trouble with full time christian missionaries in the third world at present is that they are mostly (though not quite all) white. If and when they are mostly black, brown or yellow, the question of their acceptability can become a significantly different one. It can be particularly awkward to have large numbers of American missionaries, and it is difficult to believe that the vast American missionary network in the third world is wholly unconnected, or unused by, the American CIA network in the same countries. It would be interesting to correlate the presence in third world countries of American bases (or a close political alliance) with that of missionaries.

We may turn at this point from a bird's eye view of the changing world of theology and mission over the last half century to a résumé of some general sociological laws operating in the ecumenical movement of which we need to be aware. There is, of course, nothing disgraceful about this, and there is no reason to oversimplify one's interpretation of the ecumenical movement —even of the ecumenical movement seen as a sociological phenomenon—but it would be naive to deny that the ecumenical movement as a historical reality has progressed in accordance with patterns operating in many other comparable secular situations. Here at least three forces should be recognized:

1. The tendency of declining groups to amalgamate, often on account of basic economic pressures. At the recent inauguration of an ecumenical theological training college, joining together two denominational ones, all the speeches referred to the progress this signified, the new opportunities offered, the call to unity being at last hearkened to. A priest friend who had been on the board of the chief college involved for several years remarked to me how strange it was that in all these rousing addresses not one word was said about what had in private meetings proved the decisive point: that the college had been half empty for several years, as a result the financial situation was extremely critical, and economics had simply forced some such union upon a group of people who were really anything but anxious for it. Inside the Roman Catholic Church too it is often true that co-operation between missionary societies is only achieved when a decline in numbers renders separate training programmes unviable. Such a context is not in itself the best one in which to generate an enormous new wave of missionary enthusiasm; yet it may, of course, have been quite the right decision, and one that in the new circumstances will make all the same for a more effective sense of mission than continuing apart. The Holy Spirit is as capable of using economic pressures to his final purpose as anything else. The right (though inevitably hypothetical) comparison has to be made not with the divided but flourishing conditions of earlier decades, but with what would have happened if in present circumstances things had continued divided. Institutional unification will certainly not of itself produce a renewal in mission, it may not indeed even prevent a further steady decline; but that is not to say that it does not provide a more suitable springboard, often today the only suitable springboard, for fully authentic new mission, if there is at the same time a sufficient determination.

2. It is a social and psychological fact that competition, hostility and struggle can be immensely powerful factors in keeping individuals and groups loyal to what they believe in, anxious to propagate it, willing to sacrifice and suffer for it. The less external challenge there is felt to be, the less at the natural level is the tendency to respond vigorously, to go out and witness. In the words of Katharine Whitehorn, commenting on Robert Ardrey's *The Territorial Imperative*:[33] 'People are isolated and unneighbourly: what brings them together? The outside threat of a rent rise or a motorway. Why do giant firms go soggy at the centre? Not enough abrasion from outside. Why do communal parks not satisfy the need for a personal backyard? ... once you get the message, so much becomes clear—why the Resistance, for example, that band of brothers, broke up into squabbling groups as soon as the pressure was off, or why Israel survived all those years in spite of her big angry brothers—it's the very hostility of the Arab countries that keeps her in such spanking good shape.' Of course, there are a great many points here, but it cannot be questioned that the Church is affected by the same sort of instincts. This is certainly not the only or complete explanation of why some Churches are more missionary minded than others but it is part of the explanation. A good deal of early ecumenical stimulation was strongly denominational (e.g. anti-Roman); later on it could be in terms of unity against Islam, then against Communism, or secularism and now against racialism. Competition, rivalry, even sheer fear of other religious or ideological bodies have had a great deal to do with missionary movements of the past: extremely human, but the Church is human. Nor are such attitudes wholly to be condemned. The more any clear sense of division between 'we' and 'they' dis-

[33] *Observer*, 1 February 1970, p. 17

appears, the more difficult does it undoubtedly become psychologically and sociologically to stimulate mission, the more easily do large tolerant Churches become 'soggy at the centre'. The supreme ecumenical challenge may be how to stimulate mission without falling back upon some unworthy form of competition. 3. Ours is an age of institutionalism. Even if many cry out in protest against the institutional Church, and if there is some very limited decentralization going on in the Catholic Church, there is also in all communions an almost steady growth in centralized bureaucracy, in commissions and committees of all kinds, closely parallel to the same kind of growth in government and big business. Just as in the army the ratio between people involved in supporting services and field troops is continually changing as the former group grows, so in the Church. The central offices of missionary societies are a good example. The number of the missionaries they actually field may greatly decrease, but the number of workers at headquarters still increases. Again, there are sound reasons for this. Processes of selection, training, liaison, critical evaluation of projects and so on, are all so much more complex today, and the modern obligation to a subtle complexity cannot be ignored. Nevertheless, the effect of this, especially on bodies with a totally decreasing personnel, can be extremely serious. In the ecumenical sphere it is clear how the movement for unity can become something extremely institutionalized, and appear even sterile, and this particularly in areas where there was the most hope. Even people most sensitive to this danger personally can succumb in practice. Ecumenical energies, both before and after any far-reaching unity scheme, may in fact to a disproportionate extent be engaged in internal institutional debates and readjustments. The complexity of church life, in all its aspects of doctrine, worship, ministry and mission, ensures that two groups of people anxious to join together but with variant traditions in all these fields, can discuss about their minutiae in a very creditable manner for days, months, years, and decades.

These tendencies can operate in many ways and at every level. One has experience at a very local level of situations in which the introduction of the ecumenical dimension actually kills a lively missionary initiative: the enthusiasm of a small, homogeneous denominational group anxious here and now to do a precise thing can on occasion be stifled by the broad-minded interjection that this is not a denominational matter, that it should first be discussed with representatives of other communions, that an agreed policy should be formulated on the matter, and so on. At international level it is depressing to see to what extent ecumenism can become a matter of high-powered semi-secret meetings arranged at considerable expense and increasingly issuing forth in little except repetitive and banal communiques and an agreement to undertake further meetings.

Probably most ecumenists would consider this to be a travesty of the truth. In part I believe it to be myself, but I think too that an objective sociological analysis of ecumenism can help ecumenists to be a lot more abrasively self-critical than they have been hitherto. In particular such an analysis can help to explain why the stock ecumenical claim that unity and mission go together is today questionable both at the level of fact and at the level of theology. Only if we understand the phenomenon in all its complexity, can we have much hope of correcting it in a creative way.

If missionary activity and ecumenism are thus tending to fall apart, or are at least appearing to do so, the solution must, I believe, be found firstly through a critical reappraisal both of traditional missionary activity and of modern ecumenism. It is not really that mission and unity do not go together, for it is obvious that in profound ways they do both in theology and in social psychology, but that a certain type of missionary activity does not go with a certain type of ecumenism. All Christian activities are historically conditioned and limited in the way they actually realize here and now some basic exigency of Christian life, but they can be examined and modified. The missionary activity and the ecumenism which we are considering may be each of them too one-sided, each too conditioned by a particular historical moment in which it came to maturity—the ecumenism by the angry protest movements and the 'worldly' theology of the sixties, the missionary activity by some earlier moment when a certain biblical and doctrinal fundamentalism was married to a white, western confidence in being the people of destiny called to evangelize the whole world 'in this generation'.[34] Certainly an ecumenism which either ties up its enthusiasts in endless ecclesiastical conversations or, while turning them to the world, devalues the ultimately unrivalled importance of explicit witness to Jesus Christ, is basically bad ecumenism. Equally, missionary

[34]It is noteworthy that conservative evangelicals often consider themselves the only true heirs of the old Protestant missionary movement: 'The prophet's mantle of the Edinburgh Conference has fallen on evangelical shoulders', wrote E. H. Lindsell in 1962, quoted by H. Hoekendijk, *op. cit.*, p. 27.

activity which fortifies itself with assertions which deny or practically deny the reality of God's realized love for all the millions of men far beyond the pale of the visible Church, or which considers that the word of the Bible can normally be the adequate sacrament of God's salvation almost regardless of matters of time, place and interpretation, or again which detaches the word of the *kerygma* from its earthing in the secular care of *diakonia*, is simply bad missionary activity, not faithful to the total responsibility of witnesses to the incarnate Lord.

Our duty, then, is so critically to purify both our ecumenical and our missionary activity that they cohere self-evidently as intrinsically related aspects of true discipleship in our time. In doing this, the first point is to re-assert the priority of mission. Christ came to do something, to reconcile, to proclaim, to serve. Absolute priority in the being of the disciple Church must be claimed for participation in this work of doing. We too are sent by him to proclaim, to serve, to reconcile. But such doing is impossible without a simultaneous being—the *koinonia* of Christian fellowship. Mission, God's mission which the Church is conscious that it has no other *raison d'être* than to advance, is necessarily and always an integral combination of proclamation and service, explicit witness and secular redemption, within the context of fellowship. It was so in Christ's life and it has to be so in ours. This does not mean that every place or moment is suitable for both. There may indeed be long periods when explicit witness is impossible or unsuitable—not for reasons of comfortable accommodation, but out of respect for the totality of human nature. Mission has to take the Word most seriously, but it must take the world seriously too.

Secondly, mission is impossible if there is no explicit Gospel that the bearer really believes in. I can see no future for mission or Church which is not centred upon the living Christ, identical with the historic Jesus of the Gospels who died and rose again. It may well be that Kraemer's 'Biblical realism', presented at Tambaram as a Barthian theology for mission, was very much too narrow in all sorts of ways. Certainly the tendency since has been all the other way. It would seem to me that today the Protestant ecumenical movement may be in need of a new Barthian dose, and without it mission will continue to fade away. Modern Catholic theology, which has not yet, of course, really penetrated older missionary circles, may need something similar just as much. The dimension of transcendence, of the utter uniqueness of the Christ event, of the power of the cross, of the intransigence of both Gospel and Church in their claim upon every man—these are of the *esse* of Christianity. An ecumenism which muffles these would be the faithful servant neither of God, Christ, Church or mission.

Thirdly, it is not to be gainsaid that as a matter of social fact the effectiveness of mission can be greatly impeded in many circumstances by denominational disunity, above all when the meaning of this disunity is not generally comprehensible. None can deny that a situation of missionary division, such as is described in the following passage, has weakened both the vigour of the Church's missionary workers and the meaning of their witness. It is from the 1929 report of the London Missionary Society, and I have quoted it before: 'Church work seems to progress slowly. The opposition of the Roman Catholics, the Seventh-Day Adventists, the Church of England, the Wesleyans, and the Independents, not to speak of the Ethiopians, seems to have taken much of the vigour out of the remaining workers in the LMS Church.'[35] Of course, by far the most serious effect is not a matter of diminishing the number of converts, or even producing an obvious objection for not accepting one of a number of competing alternatives, but the intrinsic effect that this sort of competition always has upon those involved, in forcing them even *malgré eux* to concentrate upon secondary but distinguishing elements in their message and in contradicting the intrinsic meaning of the fellowship they offer. Onesidedness, and even a sense of hostility to other Christians, is built into a young Church from its very foundation. It is of the nature of things that mission qualified by Christian division is affected to a greater or lesser extent in its own authenticity, because Christian unity is intrinsic to both Gospel and Church.

On the other hand, it is not surprising in the least if the achievement of limited reunion does not of itself bring about a noticeable change in missionary effectiveness. In a situation where everyone's attitude to Christianity has been conditioned, even dulled, for generations by a quantity of Christian division, it is not surprising that a limited unification should have a relatively slight immediate effect upon the deeper attitudes of either church members or non-believers. It must be remembered that in South India, for instance, the union has been very partial. The CSI does not today include even half the Christians in the area concerned. Again, a union may remain—especially in country areas—far more a matter of the leadership than of anything closely involving the mass of even active church mem-

[35] Quoted in B. A. Pauw, *Religion in a Tswana Chiefdom*, Oxford, 1960, p. 229.

bers. Further, if in countries of old Christianity reunions do not prevent a further 'decline', the answer may well be not that there is an absence of correlation between unity and mission but that there are other still more influential factors at present affecting our society which make for a decrease in religious practice, and that the reunion of communions alone (especially on what is still a small scale) is not a sufficient factor to halt that decline. The decline might have been still greater without the reunion.

I believe that if unity is sought, it must be sought with the needs of mission very consciously and continually in view. It may very well be that as a matter of hard fact reunion discussions have often paid little more than lipservice to this priority, and that subsequently they suffer the consequences. Today Roman Catholic ecumenism as a whole would seem to me to lie open to this criticism.

Perhaps the real question for us is not whether we can go on tolerating disunity, but whether we can tolerate irrelevant disunity. Disunity there must be. To deny it would really be doing a disservice to the cause of rectifying the Christian condition today. Such talk often involves a transference of truths which relate to the ultimate state of the Church, and application of them to the penultimate state. In the present, the penultimate state, there must be division of many kinds, for the penultimate state remains a fully historical condition and in human history and human society of all kinds, there always is division. It is of the nature of life *in via*. Christ himself was a bringer and a cause of division, very sharp division, and true Gospel discipleship can be continuingly divisive. There are very real divisions of belief and conduct today that it would be quite wrong to play down. Moreover, the very size of the believing community today sociologically necessitates division of many kinds. Certainly, we have partly gone wrong in too easily identifying division with a separation in ecclesiastical communion: we have to recover the sense of bearing with division inside ecclesiastical communion. But there will always remain limits to the possibility of this; some Christian divisions will still in prudent human judgement be found too considerable for ecclesiastical communion. Denial of this could really be to make it impossible for the Church to offer any communal explicit witness. There is also, deriving from the very fact of the Christ, the division between believer and non-believer. The straight application of a pattern of unity only strictly realizable in the ultimate, the new Jerusalem, to the penultimate, the here and now condition of the pilgrim

Church, can be objectively a theological naivety. The same would be true in regard to the Church's holiness. Though it is also true that it is the obligation of the Christian here and now—while recognizing the overwhelming difference between ultimate and penultimate—still to witness to the ultimate within the condition of the penultimate, and to do so precisely by erecting here and now some credible image of the ultimate.

The immediately to be striven for, historically attainable, unity of the pilgrim Church is not then to be identified with the unity of the new Jerusalem. But equally it is not to be identified with some sort of ecclesiastical uniformity, definable in contemporary terms of liturgy, church order, spirituality and theology. Either false identification can only be disastrous for the present ecumenical task, and especially for the shaping of a historically realizable future Church more manifestly both one and catholic, more seriously geared to mission, than today's. The second false identification now requires further consideration. The pluralism of the world requires a pluralism of witness, and the pluralism of witness requires a pluralism of church structures. The local Church can only be vigorously present to its own local society if it be sufficiently free to shape itself. The whole life of the Church is geared to the proclamation of the Gospel and the variety within this proclamation requires a variety in the whole range of its local structures, while at the same time the profound unity of Gospel proclamation is ensured by the profound unity of the Church. Thus the nature of the Church and its mission requires a positive acceptance of diversity to a degree that has been, and still is, completely strange to the western Roman tradition and to the practice of its central missionary organ, the congregation of *Propaganda Fide*. Work inside a specifically missionary situation in Africa or Asia makes one particularly conscious of the urgent need to break out of this. Church growth is being stifled, if not quantitatively at least qualitatively, by continued imposition of uniform patterns suitable to the northern mother Churches. This kind of imposition is so taken for granted within the Roman Catholic tradition that the Afro-Asian leaders in the young Churches have continued in many cases actually to demand it.

This does not mean, of course, that the centralized and rather monolithic practice of Catholic missionary work since the nineteenth century has been all loss. On the contrary. Rome is the missionary see *par excellence* and the fruit of her concern has been vast. The relative uniformity of Catholic missionary work has certainly not been unconnected with its quite obvious vigour and effectiveness. The mission of the Church must have a catholic, not only a local, character just as its communion must be catholic and not only local. Both require serious institutional structures at world level. The chief Roman Catholic need remains today, however, to stress the other side—a side which the Roman tradition, especially in the last 150 years, has been so very blind to.

Today ecumenism, as much as mission, requires an acceptance of pluralism. The needs of the two are, in the Roman Catholic context, strikingly the same. When we say that many of the differences between Christians have become relatively irrelevant and can no longer justify ecclesiastical separation, this does not mean that all such non-justifying differences can or should be ironed out. On the contrary. Not only would the attempt to achieve uniformity make union between Roman Catholics, Anglicans, Lutherans and Methodists humanly impossible, at least for a very long time, but it would, of course, be a most terrible impoverishment. The Holy Spirit has worked in all these Churches, and all have their own inherited riches. Moreover, as a matter of fact, given the growing Roman insistence in recent centuries upon uniformity at all levels, it was perhaps only the break of communion that really enabled these riches to develop. While the break was in itself bad, it has actually helped to protect much that was good and which could easily have been destroyed or never had the freedom to develop if there had been no break: as witness the deplorable Romanization of both Irish and English Catholicism in the nineteenth century. (This was, of course, especially in the case of Ireland, enormously helped by the secular political pressure upon the old Irish Church, a state of continued persecution which had resulted in a rather structureless local Church only too open to the importation of a foreign ecclesiastical culture.)

What is alarming today is that Protestant ecumenists over the last half century or more in rediscovering and stressing the Catholic principle that division (schism) is sinful, seem in danger of forgetting the Protestant principle that division (sectarianism) is fruitful. Catholics too, who have plunged into the same tide, are increasingly asking: are such divisions as those between religious orders not somehow wrong? Aren't they dangerously 'divisive'? Should we not all be as one as we can be? I can think of nothing more disastrous than such a line of thought. Unity can only be spiritually authentic in a time-space context, humanly tolerable, continuingly fruitful and evangelically powerful if it is mediated through diversity and a diversity which is sufficiently genuine to provoke tension and deep disagreement.

Ecumenists have done far too little to work out what this really means. At least until they have done so the present chaotic denominational division plus much friendly co-operation may be greatly preferable to the monochrome uniformity which unity would be likely to produce.

The greatest immediate question to be put to the ecumenical movement (and particularly to those who officially represent the movement in the Roman Catholic communion) is how reunion is not, effectively, to be destructive of legitimate diversity. Ecumenists constantly, and sincerely, declare that they are working for unity, not uniformity. Nevertheless the very elements of the problem are against them. In practice many ecumenical discussions turn largely on attaining some sort of uniformity—in prayer forms, lectionaries, the formulation of doctrine, the balance of laity and clergy in decision making, even the date of Easter. There is indeed an obvious temptation, when major issues of division seem irreducible, to stave off discouragement by producing agreement on some quite unnecessary measure of uniformity in areas where pluriformity is in fact eminently fitting. A striking example of this is the recurring campaign to establish a single fixed date for Easter. Nothing is much more irrelevant, indeed more opposed to true ecumenism. It is really just one more example of the willingness of the church's shepherds to sell out to the pressures of the world—responding, not to the true secular needs of ordinary human beings, but to the uniformity mongers of international capitalism.

The trouble becomes that much greater when full unity of communion ('organic unity') is agreed upon. The arguments for common ministerial training, a uniform liturgy and so forth become irresistible and as a result diverse traditions (especially the small ones) almost inevitably disintegrate. Of course, in the Church too there has to be death as well as life; some things must die even though there be nothing wrong about them. Evidently also effective mission and fellowship will not be achieved locally by Christians even if they are united in ecclesiastical communion, if they are divided in so many other ways. The position of having a multiplicity of rites in communion with one another in a single place—as we see it in the Catholic Church in Lebanon, South India and elsewhere—is certainly far from an ideal one. Unity of witness and service at local level generally requires a considerable unity in the other dimensions of church life. If this is so, it becomes still truer that the wealth of diverse church traditions, subsistent today in divided communions, can only not be lost if a much greater diversity is accepted between different local Churches, so that in different places different traditions, or combinations of tradition, will predominate within the united Church of the future. The alternative would be a fantastic impoverishment which would in fact cripple the Church precisely in its missionary function as in its sacramental character of being the sign of the renewed humanity, as rich and diverse as the humanity it informs.

If we really see all this, I think we can realize better the profound dangers inherent in a centralized ecumenism. The latter is, of course, a temptation for all communions in this modern centralizing world, but it is a particular temptation for Roman Catholicism, and it is one to which, at official instigation and command, we are in danger of succumbing. The very zeal and determination of the Secretariat for the Promotion of Christian Unity, operating largely and almost inevitably according to the centralized Roman curial tradition, can become a factor actually harmful to an ecumenism which could really reunite the diverse traditions of today and—still more important—fashion a missionary Church for the future. Cardinal Willebrands has certainly shown his personal awareness of this problem in his fine sermon at Great St Mary's, Cambridge, in January 1970. Nevertheless in practice the problem and the danger, grounded in the depths of the Roman ecclesiastical tradition, remain extremely real and it would be truly tragic if an increasingly curial World Council of Churches played up to us in this matter. Protestants will not help Catholics at this juncture if they forget to remain Protestants. Only in a context of far greater decentralization (and this must be effective not only at the formal level of ecumenical activity, but at the levels of theological training, ministerial structure, liturgical worship, missionary society and much else) is it possible to think within the context of the Christianity of the 1970s of realizing unity for the sake of mission. The alternatives are either no unity at all, or a unity which could seriously impede mission. It would be better to continue with less unity and more mission, than to have more organizational unity and less mission.

That the attitude towards mission must change as much as attitudes towards unity is absolutely true. It is clear that it is not simply modern ecumenism which is cutting the ground from under certain nineteenth-century attitudes to mission but so very much else in the modern Church and the modern world. Indeed, in more and more circumstances, it is only ecumenism which can provide a new ground for mission: effective mission—whether evangelism or service—is often simply inconceivable today in a non-ecumenical form. Equally, when unity in mission is realized, continued division in communion becomes more and more intolerable and indeed meaningless. Rather than to say that we must have unity in communion in order to be united in mission, it is sounder to say that a growing unity in mission will be the decisive spur to unity in communion. Today above all the mission-minded cannot dispense with the search for unity nor ignore the central insights gained in the long journey from Edinburgh to Uppsala. If one is to be open to the claims both of the whole Gospel and the whole world one can only accept the central options that, in Protestant terms, are signified in the career of Oldham, in the integration of the IMC into the WCC, in most of what was agreed and published at Uppsala, and finally in the Programme for Combatting Racism and the grants for non-military purposes to the liberation movements.

It has to be admitted in conclusion that Catholic missionary history in this century seems very simple at the level of ideas in comparison with Protestant. Until the last few years there was very little questioning of purposes and no serious division about the theological interpretation of doctrine. On the one side Catholic missionary work was never so spiritual, so 'pure' as much Protestant work tried to be; there was nearly always a strong social concern. On the other hand there was almost no political concern. Cardinal Lavigerie's political crusade for the ending of slavery was a vast exception. Almost nowhere did Catholic missionaries think that it was their duty in some way to challenge the injustices of colonialism and racialism, as a good many Protestants have done. When we, like our Protestant brothers, choose this option today as an integral element of mission, we cannot point back as they can to prophets of the recent past. Hence, too, we have not until these last few years heard the cry that the purity of the Gospel is being betrayed by the breadth of our concern or the modernism of our theology— the old modernism never affected the missionary movement. Nevertheless in Catholic terms too the new option is now clear. It is that signified by the encyclical *Populorum Progressio*, by the Conciliar Declaration on non-Christian religions, by Bede Griffiths in his Indian ashram, by the White Fathers who withdrew from Mozambique, and the Burgos Fathers who remained there in prison, by Archbishop Helder Camara.

The alternative for all of us would be a mutilated Gospel. But it is also true that the ecumenism of today and all that goes with it can wound mission and will do so unless, first, the need for unity and central organisations of a sort are harmonized with the need for pluralism to an extent far beyond anything the leadership of the Latin Church has yet contemplated; secondly, the stress on human development in all its forms, personal, social and political, immediate liberation, is integrated with but in no way substituted for the proclamation of an explicit gospel of ultimate liberation: the one being indeed the sacrament and vehicle of the other. Thirdly, that this explicit gospel be interpreted across an adequately sophisticated hermeneutic, which does not nevertheless denude it of its central content—the 'scandal' of the incarnation, the historic time-space particularity of Jesus Christ, son of the Father, crucified and risen, the reconciler.

It seems likely that these are in fact the very priorities today of the churches of the southern hemisphere which are more and more coming to pull their weight within world christianity both Protestant and Catholic. Uppsala with all its strengths and weaknesses was probably the last World Council of Churches event to be dominated by the North Atlantic churches, despite the already notable increase in non-European representation, in contrast with the character of the fifth assembly (Nairobi, November 1975), a predominantly Afro/Asian/South American gathering. There has been a growing break-through in the ecclesiastical map of influence, confidence and representation these last years. By and large the churchmen of the 'third world' appear no more interested than Uppsala in a 'pure gospel' of the Frankfurt Declaration type—a gospel disembodied from the contemporary task of human liberation. In this they have little sympathy with the strict conservative evangelical, whether German or Anglo-Saxon. But, equally, they are little interested in a demythologized gospel or a refusal to evangelize. The subtle intricacies of western theologizing these last two decades, much of it sterile enough, has mostly passed them by. Here their sympathies are far closer to conservative evangelicals. They are willing enough to take up the prophet's mantle of the Edinburgh Conference, and will need to beware its lining of triumphalism. Their influence in Nairobi at this juncture may be decisive for the coming direction of the world ecumenical movement.

7

The present state of the ecumenical movement and reciprocal intercommunion

Where does the ecumenical movement go now? The churches must undoubtedly work more and more together in mission, but at the same time they must grow closer together in fellowship—indeed, the one is impossible without the other. While they grow together in fellowship the walls of institutional separation will inevitably crumble and all that is living on each side coalesce. But just how is this to happen? The question is an intensely practical one because the quest of the last few decades for 'organic unity', the quest which achieved the Church of South India, the United Church of Zambia, the Church of North India, and which produced the Anglican/Methodist scheme in England, that quest has seemed these last few years less and less profitable. Its achievement is fair enough when rather small bodies are concerned, and there are places where schemes for organic unity of the type we have known can still be pursued with profit. The 1972 merger of Congregationalists and Presbyterians in England in the new United Reformed Church is an obvious example. But as a model of ecumenical unity it grows more and more cumbersome, the larger the scale of the churches involved or the more numerous they are.

Personally while in some ways very sad that the Anglican/ Methodist scheme was finally rejected in 1972, I was in other ways relieved. I do not believe that this kind of scheme is really the best way forward today, and the Methodist voice is so characteristic and still so important in England that I would absolutely not wish it to be somehow muffled or absorbed within the present folds of the established church. The free churches, Catholics of the Roman communion and the established tradition will one day come together to rebuild the unity of 'Ecclesia Anglicana' shattered four centuries ago, but the time is not quite yet.

The basic reason why at present organic unity is not a reasonable primary objective for ecumenical effort is not, however, its cumbersomeness—round which a way will in due course be found —but that one still cannot see the likelihood of its including Roman Catholics, and yet no plan which excludes Roman Catholics can any more be very satisfactory for anyone. The schemes for organic unity we have known grew up at a time before Catholics were taking ecumenism seriously; they were essentially an inter-Protestant way forward. Today, however, Catholics are in so many ways central to the ecumenical movement that projects which do not include them will not raise much enthusiasm even among non-Roman Catholics, though there are undoubtedly many people, even among the pundits, who have not yet quite seen the implication of this—just as there are many Catholics who will still urge that such schemes go forward, precisely because they continue to see themselves as somewhat marginal to the whole enterprise.

Those of us who do not believe in that particular type of marginality but believe that the re-establishment of a viable visible communion of christians of the Roman Catholic, Orthodox, Anglican and Protestant traditions really is a possibility in our time—and a possibility imposing upon us an intense and continuing moral obligation—have for the present to seek another way. That other way I believe to be a steady growth in co-operation at all levels, but a growth which is not at this stage ordered, institutionalized or defined. It must be a growth in every aspect of christian living—proclamation, secular service, human fellowship, prayer. It is a growth realized through the sharing of church buildings and the merging of pastoral structures, the sharing of retreats and theological conferences, the sharing of inter-church marriage. More and more this is in fact happening, but as it happens it presents in each circumstance the dilemma of joining or not joining in that central moment of prayer, fellowship and proclamation, the 'sacrament of unity', eucharistic communion. Today intercommunion is without doubt the most important internal issue facing the ecumenical movement—intercommunion between Catholics and others. It cannot and must not be bypassed anymore. Out of its responsible growth within the context of a wider shared Christian faith, life and mission will grow the full unity of the Church of the 1980s. Our organic unity can now hardly come by 1980, but it can come I am convinced, if we cannot yet envisage the precise way, before 1990 so long as we do not shirk this immediate and admittedly difficult hurdle. The organic unity we are pressing forward towards (an organic unity which will take different institutional forms in different parts of the

96

world) will give us a more catholic communion than we have ever known; it will include, as always, its Petrine ministry—a papacy renewed, humbled but not humiliated, loved more widely than it has ever been—but it will include also the heirs of the Reformation, humbled too but not humiliated, enlightening the whole of the *Catholica* with insights of which it should never have been so largely deprived; the Greeks, the Copts, the Russians, they can all be there. Yet this is not the vision of the eschaton, of ultimate bliss, but a vision of the practicable call of our generation, if we be but faithful, generous and persevering. If we do not leave things to the ecclesiastical bureaucrats.

But it is not a vision of the next five years. The immediate way forward is through the practicabilities of inter-church marriage, church sharing and such like, but above all through a steady advance in intercommunion. With the Windsor Agreement on the Eucharist behind us, this is particularly opportune today as between Catholics and Anglicans, and it is with this in mind that I include here my own personal response to the question: Is there room today for reciprocal intercommunion between Catholics and Anglicans? It was first addressed to a group of Anglican and Roman Catholic theologians meeting in June 1973 at Salamanca.

When after ordination in 1955 it was decided that I should stay on in Rome to obtain a doctorate and I looked round for a suitable subject for my thesis I settled upon that of a comparison between the Roman Catholic and Anglican concepts of church unity. I felt from the start that the basic ecclesiological issue was not one concerning the papacy but about what sort of a body the church essentially is. I narrowed the Anglican field to limit it to modern Anglo-Catholic writers from Gore on—Dom Gregory Dix, Archbishop Ramsey, Professor Mascall. Under the influence of the writings of Abbot (now Bishop) Christopher Butler and Fr Henry St John I wished to try to put my finger on the basic dividing issue between two conceptions and show, of course, that the Anglican conception was finally untenable. Where so much was held in common the issue I was sure related to the ultimate reason why Catholics could not admit that the visible church was larger than the Roman Catholic communion while Anglicans could accept that the visible church existed within a number of separated communions. My point of departure was really various articles of Butler in the *Downside Review* in which he argued very forcibly that the Church is essentially a visible society or association and that whatever the Roman Catholic and Anglican communions are today they are not one association; hence at least one of them must be separated *from* the Church. Basically schism is from the Church, rather than within. As I worked on with this idea, my view of it became both clearer and somewhat different from that with which I began. This was surely due to the influence both of continental theologians such as Frs Congar and De Lubac and of some of the Anglican theologians whom I, a very confident young man, had set out to refute. The Church on earth I recognized still as a visible association of a sort, one however of a very special kind, an association which has traditionally been given the name of communion. It is in its internally ordered structure essentially a eucharistic association. It is here, I discovered, that its unbreakable unity in the visible order is to be found. 'By the unity of communion ... the Church is one' Dom Gregory wrote in a very perceptive essay on the ancient liturgies published in 1937. When I read that sentence I was sure that it was true. Basically it is through communion or intercommunion (and the latter word has been used in the past to mean quite the same as the former, only it suggests the communion of communions—the relationship between local congregations or churches, entities with a corporate reality of their own) that the Church is one, that she is herself. The church is a communion: that was my central personal discovery. My doctoral work was completed and defended in 1958; it was published with little alteration in its main thesis under the title of *One and Apostolic* in 1963. While its vision, I remain convinced fifteen years later, was an absolutely right one, and it was surely confirmed by the documents of the second Vatican Council, its adequate concretization within the complexity of human ecclesial experience through the ages is a far more subtle matter than I then acknowledged. But I can at least claim that I have somehow been struggling with the ecclesial implications of eucharistic communion and the eucharistic implications of ecclesial communion ever since the 1950s. Like many other people, however, it has been during the last ten years that I have had to attempt ever more personally the reconciliation of a Catholic vision of the Church of the kind I have outlined with the continuing experience of a religious and Christian situation in which deep ecclesiastical divisions are clear enough but where it seems less and less satisfactory, either theologically or practically, simply to 'unchurch' the other side. I have been forced to struggle with this through membership of the Joint Anglican/Roman Catholic preparatory commission from January 1967 to January 1968, and subsequently through years of shared work, worship and witness at Mindolo

Ecumenical Foundation in Zambia, as commissioned by the Anglican archbishops of Africa to study their marriage discipline, as a visiting lecturer at Lincoln Theological College and as a tutor at the College of the Ascension on the ecumenical campus of Selly Oak. Through these years I have time and time again been faced with the issue of intercommunion in a wide variety of circumstances. I have tried continually to be loyal both to the Catholic vision of the Church as a communion-society and to the urgent exigencies of the human situation, the spiritual, pastoral and missionary needs which I have encountered. Ten years ago I still thought any form of intercommunion between members of our divided churches quite out of the question; five years ago I could see how in occasions of emergency we could receive Anglicans to Catholic communion, but was still unready to go further than that—I was actually influenced by the predominantly anti-intercommunion attitude I sensed among members of the joint preparatory commission. Within these last years my own views have changed a good deal more, largely—I think—because I have realized that the *de facto* ecclesial situation is, already now, considerably different from that which I and most Catholics used to conceive it to be: the ecclesial status of the eastern orthodox—their position as we Catholics recognize it to be rather than their own theology, though that is important too—forces one to modify the rather hard outlines of the accepted Roman Catholic position, and once that is done, I have been able to see no reason not to apply that modification *mutatis mutandis* also to our western divisions.

I have, consequently, found it possible and indeed necessary to interpret the old vision with a vastly new flexibility. I may be deluding myself but I do not think that my ecclesiology has radically altered since completing my thesis on 'The unity of the Church and Anglo-Catholicism' in 1958 and yet my view both of the ecclesial reality of the Anglican communion and of the possibility and desirability of intercommunion within our present situation has immensely changed. By 1970 I had come to the conclusion that Catholics can and even should receive Anglican communion in some exceptional circumstances and late in 1971 I found myself within a situation which seemed to call for it, and I did so for the first time. Psychologically it was far from being an easy thing to do. Since then I have become increasingly convinced that while the time has not yet arrived for general intercommunion, yet we should not be so restrictive in our approach to the question, that it is not just a matter of the personal emergency but the overall right thing to do in a number of circumstances, and that it may now be that those who refuse intercommunion rather than those who call for it have the onus on proving their case. In an article in *One in Christ* for January 1971 I endeavoured to put forward a cautious case for some intercommunion; and in a further article published in January 1973 I argued for a somewhat bolder strategy, accepting that a fully Catholic ecclesiology which has at its heart the eucharist/Church relationship—if understood with the proper historical dimensions of a real people of God in time and space—both justifies and calls for a steady growth in intercommunion between Roman Catholics, Anglicans and other christians in the circumstances of today; that growth of this kind is a necessary part of the reunion process, and that we could be faithless to our ecumenical vocation if in all circumstances we continued to hold back from such a course.

Let me first suggest that, while sharing eucharistic communion is most clearly something of immense importance within the total Christian programme of life, it is not the only or the supreme value. That may be obvious enough when it is said, but it needs saying. It is, after all, in the line of sacrament; is it not, as such, in the line of the signified. At the level of sacrament, the eucharist is indeed the full sacrament of Christ and the Church as nothing else is, but its very importance can only be properly appreciated if it is conceived within the order to which it belongs and with the qualities which that order requires. Its celebrations must be authentic (that is consonant with its own integral meaning) and opportune. It is not opportune for a sacrament to be celebrated when the sick need to be tended or even vegetables planted or a game of cricket played or the scriptures meditated. Again, when the time is convenient, it would not be authentic to celebrate the eucharist if those doing it have not a common sense of what the eucharist really is, or want to make of it what it is not. It would be wonderful to be in eucharistic communion with everyone on earth, but not unless everyone on earth themselves wanted it with some adequate sense of what it is they are wanting. All things considered we cannot say that God's will within the foreseeable future is that all men should be in eucharistic communion with one another, because this presupposes their being believing christians, and it is not clear that it is God's will that all men should so be—at least in our time. It is not even self-evident that all men within the christian tradition should be in communion with one another. The obligation to share the eucharist together is a very strong one but it does not ride roughshod over all other obligations; in life there are a multiplicity of religious and moral demands made upon one; some of these demands conflict or seem to conflict with one another. In our quest to share eucharistic communion we must not short-circuit other issues. Nobody has a right to say *a priori* that the obligation for Christians to share the Lord's supper together necessarily takes precedence over every other demand, if in the minds of some it really is held to conflict with another obligation. Nevertheless we have a right, I think, to ask very seriously if there really be such a conflict; that we do not easily admit the over-ruling of one major obligation by others.

If the eucharist is indeed the sacrament of unity, we must admit that it does not exclude an intrinsic divisiveness, just as the gospel itself is divisive, as the Church is divisive. This is a paradox but not one to be brushed aside. Its divisiveness is not merely a matter of human frailty, or—if it is—it is because human frailty itself is built into the constitution of the world and even of the Church. Within human society things exclude divisiveness only if they are trivial or vague or obvious or non-committing. Almost everything else is deeply divisive in one way or another, and the more important a message or a mission is the more divisive its effect must be for those who do not, or will not, or cannot accept it. This is really a sociological law, and the sacrament of unity is itself subject to it—just as the Lord Jesus was, and the gospel continuously is. In an official Marxist atheist society the Christian Church is evidently a divisive agency; in some other societies this may be slightly less evident, but it is not less true. There are Christians today who would base their appeal for intercommunion on a view of the eucharist as necessarily a completely open, non-divisive reality, available to the non-baptized, the non-christian, the non-interested. It may well be that it is unnecessary and even harmful to have a discipline of exclusion, that the intrinsic exclusiveness of the eucharist can be left to work of itself, but I believe that it should not be doubted that the eucharist, despite being sacrament of unity, still partakes in principle of the divisiveness of the gospel, of the faith commitment of a limited fellowship. It has an inclusiveness entailing an exclusiveness which is not to be gainsaid, and it is not *a priori* obvious just where and how the line is to be drawn. To deny its divisiveness and exclusiveness would finally be to destroy its very existence as a bearer of significant, indeed unique, meaning, and it would be to reject next to the whole Christian eucharistic tradition we are heirs to. As a concrete event the eucharist grows out of the upper room not out of the hillside. I presuppose that any acceptable argument for intercommunion should be consonant with this tradition and not imply the transformation of the *mysterium fidei* into something, a meal of absolutely unqualified openness, which in tradition and meaning it has never been. These are very general considerations but they do, I believe, have their importance if the argument for intercommunion is not to be misconceived.

The Church is the fellowship on earth of believing Christians and finds its focal point, its regular reason for associating, its cause and interpretative celebration of being what it is, in the Eucharist. The body of Christ, it makes those who share in it to be the body of Christ; the blood of the new covenant, it makes those who share in it to be the new people of God; communion meal, it makes those who share in it to be a communion. It does not do all this apart from the word of God, faith, baptism, the grace of the Holy Spirit; but it is the central sacrament which within the corporate and personal life of Christians affirms, strengthens and manifests the totality of what God has done in Christ and what ecclesial life is about. This fellowship is entered into by baptism which specifically makes people members of the eucharistic communion, and it is served by a variety of ministries, particularly the episcopal/presbyteral ministry whose task it is to preside over the eucharistic celebration itself.

The eucharistic fellowship is in a real primary sense a local fellowship because the eucharist is necessarily a local event and only fully sacrament at that level. But the unity of eucharist as the unity of baptism reflects the unity of Christ and guarantees the unity of local Churches in one Church, and this in its turn is reflected and guarded by the unity of ministries ensured by hierarchical communion.

Throughout the history of the Church this full unity of communion has time and again been threatened, partially broken or wholly broken by divisions, by schisms, sometimes personal quarrels, sometimes conflicts within the hierarchy or between local Churches, sometimes divisions over doctrine, the basic sense of the faith. These divisions breach the fullness of communion to a varying degree, leaving people within a partial communion of more or less extent. Sometimes they have done little more than upset personal or group relations; sometimes they have institutionally disrupted hierarchical communion but hardly affected eucharistic communion; sometimes they have damaged the latter indeed but not fully broken it; sometimes they have entirely broken eucharistic communion but left still in existence fellowship in the one baptism and credal faith; sometimes they have damaged or destroyed even this. What degree of communion remains, it is always as such communion within the Church; but in so far as communion is ruptured the rupture may be contained within the body of Christ, but of its nature it tends to separate at least some people from the fullness of Catholic living, and as the visible Church is in its central functioning a eucharistic fellowship, a full break at the level of eucharist is of its nature a break from, rather than within, the fellowship of the Church.

Our main task within any situation of division is not, however, to analyse and assess degrees of Church membership but to restore the fullness of fellowship in unity: steadily to increase the degree of communion, to lessen the degree of division: to make the Church of here and now and those who have been baptized into her the manifest sacrament of unity which she essentially and eschatologically is but historically has partially failed to be.

There is a certain internal necessity in the progress of the ecumenical movement which reflects the deeply unitary nature of the Church and all that relates to her. The communion of the Church is an integral reality; each aspect of it is linked with every other so that once one admits sharing a partial but not full communion, one has to admit that one is within an essentially anomalous situation, a condition of internal contradiction, in which the here and now institutional Church does not fully correspond with what we believe her to be and claim that she is. This state is not, of course, characteristic of the post-Reformation condition only; it has been deeply true of almost every previous age as well and it can be true of particular historical situations because it is true in a still deeper way of the historical Church as such: the Church, as she is, is not the Church as she should be, as we indeed profess her—and rightly profess her—to be. In some way we profess our belief already in the eschatological Church, the Church as she will be and should be, and is by the power of the Holy Spirit on her way to being. The Church now can never wholly fail to be herself and yet she can greatly fail and does indeed in some sense necessarily fail to be all that she should be. The condition of the historical Church is really a condition of continual anomaly, at times sensed more, at others less; always to be struggled with, never to be denied. The anomaly of partial communion is a manifestation of the inescapable anomaly of a church which in time is a sinful people being, becoming, therefore in some way not yet being, the body of Christ.

We are in an anomalous, an imperfect, a messy situation. The accepted Roman Catholic position has laid great stress upon the intrinsic relationship between hierarchical communion and eucharistic communion; it has been right to do so. But it is necessary to lay an equal stress—and perhaps finally give an even greater weight to—the intrinsic relationship between eucharistic communion and baptismal communion; between, indeed, Christian faith and eucharist, the sacrament of faith; to admit the grave abnormality of recognizing fellow Christians but excluding them from one's eucharistic faith communion. We have accepted the validity and unity of our common baptism; in doing so we have, I suspect, accepted a time bomb whose eucharistic explosion cannot now be long delayed. Our one baptism is of its nature entry into one common Church and if the one and only Church is as we claim it to be—of its nature a eucharistic communion, the body of Christ fed upon the body of Christ, then in accepting a common baptism we have accepted a common passport to the eucharistic table of the Lord; it is not clear that this passport, to be valid, also requires an additional hierarchical visa. In the very clear words of St Thomas Aquinas: 'Per baptismum ordinatur homo ad Eucharistiam' (S. Theol. III, 73 : 3). By baptism a man is brought up into relationship with the eucharist and the eucharistic community: he becomes a member of the latter and already receives by desire the intrinsic fruit of the former, the fullness of Christian and ecclesial communion. In accepting Anglican baptism the Catholic communion has recognised that an Anglican has in principle a full right to receive a full, true, Catholic Eucharist to which the one valid baptism is *per se* related. But one does not have the right to receive communion only on one's own; the reception of the eucharist is of its nature a communal event, communion is intercommunion: one eucharist, one catholic communion. Ordered to the eucharist, we are ordered to the eucharistic community, and we have an intrinsic right to participate in the latter—to stand or kneel beside our brothers and sisters in the faith receiving the body and blood of the Lord.

Certainly the Catholic communion is a fellowship of local churches and eucharistic communion is primarily a local event. One enters in baptism into a local community first. It is perfectly proper that there should be rules of courtesy and caution to be followed in moving from one local church to another, and these certainly had great weight in the early Church. But they must not be used to negate the primary sense of the unity of Church, baptism and Lord's supper.

The baptized have a right to intercommunicate. More and more that seems to me a central ecclesiological assertion, which we can only tamper with at our peril. The right to intercommunion is not bestowed by Church authority, it is given by the nature of the Church and the baptism/eucharist relationship; it may indeed be lost, but that only for good reason. It cannot simply be taken away. Hence if we, accepting one another's baptism, cannot or should not share communion together, then we have to find adequate reason to justify our reneging upon this extremely important dimension of our baptismal commitment. We do not in fact need further to justify intercommunion; what we have to justify is the refusal to intercommunicate here and now.

Sufficient reasons there can be. They can, I think, take three forms. Firstly, lack of common belief. The one baptism signifies a unity in basic belief; if this is not in fact a reality, one cannot honestly celebrate and proclaim it. A decisive inability to agree upon what one is doing when one eucharistizes must undermine the meaningfulness of a common action. Secondly, personal, moral or communal divisions can be of such a character as to undermine the necessary foundation and realizable significance of the celebration of the sacrament. Thirdly, one may be unable to accept a particular minister or group of ministers as possessing the necessary qualities for the office of presiding over the eucharist. Let us consider each of these three.

The eucharist is the *mysterium fidei*, the central sacrament of Christian life which praises God in proclaiming and making present the full saving reality of Jesus Christ through his body the Church. If Christians believe this, they wish to share this sacrament only with those who believe it too. We are members of many fellowships and will express this in other ways and by other means. We simply disembowel the eucharist, whose meaning is not chiefly to be found in a friendly breaking of bread but in the breaking of bread which is the body of Christ, dead and risen, if we enact it apart from a community of belief. It is true that every man of good will if he is to be saved has somehow in him saving faith, though he may have no conscious knowledge or acceptance of the redeemer. But we must distinguish here between faith and belief.[1] Belief is explicit and conscious. The eucharist is not only sacrament of faith in the wider sense, it is

[1] Reference can be made here to the study of Nicholas Lash on *Credal Affirmation as a Criterion of Church Membership*, in *Intercommunion and Church Membership*, edited by John Kent and Robert Murray, S.J., London, 1973.

the sacrament and focal point of a community of belief, involving deliberate response to an intellectually highly significant form of words. The identification of this bread and this wine with the body and blood of Christ, inaugurating a covenant, shed for sins, can make no sense and can therefore be but hocuspocus outside the united circle of explicit Christian belief.

Unity of belief is never absolute in the sense of an identical common understanding of what we believe. Even when accepting a wholly common formula within a single organic communion people will not really understand it in quite the same way. Community of belief inevitably shares in the ambiguity of all human understanding and communication. Yet human beings are able in a rational way to convince themselves that there does exist a substantial agreement or disagreement upon this point or that. In the Church we have done this traditionally by means of brief statements called creeds whose honest acceptance leaves vast room for deep differences of understanding and interpretation. How much conflict and disagreement in explicit belief can justify the refusal to intercommunicate? By admitting Eastern Orthodox to Catholic communion and Catholics to Orthodox communion in a wide variety of cases the second Vatican Council and the subsequent Ecumenical Directory have confirmed much traditional practice and indicated that some serious disagreement in the range and articulation of belief is still compatible with the sharing of eucharistic communion. The degree of unity in belief properly required would seem to be most logically controlled by the nature of that which is being done; and this too appears to be the view of the Secretariat of Unity. What is precisely needed for sharing the supper of the Lord is an adequate unity of christological belief somehow concretized in and about the eucharistic event. What we are looking for is not precisely credal unity, although this is presupposed and somehow included, but rather that of the eucharistic prayer itself. For surely the canon is precisely an adequate statement of faith, in traditional doxological form, for the worshipping community within this situation. We do not ask participants to sign the canon in advance, but it is to be presumed that if one comes to Mass and receives communion one accepts the belief affirmations of the canon; indeed the people's 'Amen' to the canon after the great doxology records the explicit acceptance of this prayer in faith. If one can say 'Amen' with a good and informed conscience at the end of the canon, then I would conclude one cannot be properly excluded from communion on account of belief. Those who cannot do so will naturally exclude themselves as people were already doing in the time of Ignatius of Antioch: 'They abstain from eucharist and prayer because they allow not that the eucharist is the flesh of our Saviour Jesus Christ, which flesh suffered for our sins and which the Father of his goodness raised up' (Smyrneans, 6). They withdrew from communion because their christological-eucharistic unity of belief was inadequate.

The Secretariat of Unity has clearly affirmed that the substantial unity of eucharistic belief existing between Catholics and Orthodox is a major reason why it is possible to share communion across this divide rather easily. The Roman Catholic/Anglican Commission in its Windsor Statement of 1971 has declared that the same unity of belief is to be found between the Anglican communion and the Catholic communion. The statement has been so widely welcomed by bishops and theologians that it would indeed appear to represent a consensus, and the rapid authorization of its publication by the Pope personally is also highly significant. Beyond this one may simply compare recent eucharistic prayers in the two communions, for example the new Latin canons and series II and III. While it could well be argued that the gap in meaning between the old Latin canon and the 1662 prayer book was profound, it can hardly be denied that our new eucharistic prayers are doxologically affirming the same thing and that he who can say 'Amen' to the one can sincerely do so also to the other.

To move to our second area of possible difficulty. The local Church gathers men and women here and now to celebrate the Lord's supper. The eucharist is the cause, focal point, explaining medium of their whole life. If one is unable to participate in that wider life, then it can become meaningless and wrong to participate in the eucharistic celebration. Of course one may be a visitor, a welcome stranger, or a weak member gladly borne with, but there are situations in which—despite possible unity in formal faith—unity of communion is no longer appropriate or even morally possible. It would be a farce if one is at the same time deliberately and systematically segregated in life and mission. If one is to proclaim here together, break the bread here together, one must—at least to some credible extent—behave elsewhere as a united witnessing and serving fellowship. If one has ceased to be the latter, then one should not share the eucharist together either. That was really what happened in the sixteenth century: one fellowship slowly broke apart and became two or more. It would have been quite inappropriate to maintain some sort of bare eucharistic intercommunion when its matrix within the communion of the society had not merely been threatened but systematically removed. This did not, however, take place in a day. In England there was still some sort of common ecclesiastical society with some amount of sharing in eucharistic communion well into Elizabeth's reign. But the logic of the movement within the situation finally brought it to an end. And so we remained until very recently. Up to twenty years ago this was surely of itself an adequate reason for refusing intercommunion between Anglicans and Roman Catholics in at least ninety-nine cases out of a hundred. It remains so in the majority of cases but in a growing number of circumstances it is now simply not so. We are on the contrary sharing anew in a wider Christian community of work and worship which calls for eucharistic intercommunion rather than segregation. The logic of the movement within today's situation is arguing the other way. Far from feeling that our human and community relations make eucharistic sharing an impossibility, we find that on an increasing number of occasions they are loudly calling for it lest we make of the eucharist an occasion, bastion and sacrament of segregation within a group of Christian believers otherwise strongly aware of their unity. If we could not in the past psychologically get ourselves to say any prayers together, except on the rarest of occasions, we were obviously not remotely ready for sharing this most central of prayers; if today we regularly pray together we have already re-created the spiritual environment in which intercommunion is meaningful and its refusal requires to be painfully justified.

Our third type of difficulty concerns lack of acceptability in a minister. Clearly in an individual and exceptional case it might be because of the man himself—a betrayer of the Church, an admitted agnostic, an open sadist, a torturer, an oppressor of God's poor. One could share with the community as a whole but to accept this man's presidency over it is an unholy, a morally impossible thing to do. One could do the same because of his clear lack of authorization, even though he was once ordained in ever so valid a manner: here and now his ministry is itself dividing the Church and it is better to refuse to communicate with his little schismatic or semi-schismatic congregation. Again one may have deep doubts about his ordination, the manner in which it was done, the man who did it, particularly if this took place at a time of wide disturbance within the Church. Such, of course, is the Roman *gravamen* against Anglican orders, and no one has a right to scorn or treat such an objection lightly. The Church's continual care for the fullness of the 'traditio' of her life and doctrine is far too important for that. However one may ultimately define the character of the priestly ministry and the meaning and significance of 'valid' orders, it is clear without doubt that from very early times the Church has been extremely careful as to the passing on of the presbyteral/episcopal ministry, and we have no right at all to turn impatiently from this long and careful tradition and the deep pastoral concern that underlies it.

If high authority within one's Church declares the orders of a certain group of ministers doubtful or invalid, it is an extremely sound reason for withdrawing from the eucharist that they administer. Let us note at once that this provides a one way difficulty: Anglicans in no way challenge the adequacy of the orders of Roman Catholic priests, so this particular objection does not arise when there is only a question of receiving Anglicans to Catholic communion. In a very real way, therefore, it is not an objection to sharing communion as such. Questions of ministry are not on the same level as those of communion and intercommunion. Nevertheless in practice it is of the greatest importance. Experience within such situations convinces one of this. Moreover it is closely linked with the wider ecclesial recognition of the Churches of the Anglican communion. What then can be said in this matter? It is very clear that the Roman condemnation of Anglican orders was not an infallible or finally irrevocable decision although it certainly was a solemn and serious one. It is widely agreed today that there are ample grounds, theological and historical, on which the case can and should be reopened and I personally continue to hope that this will be done soon and in a fully joint manner. But on the most favourable supposition a public official decision of recognition could hardly be made for some time. In the meantime very deep shifts of emphasis in the theology of the ministry, the Eucharist and the Church have undoubtedly undermined quite considerably the overall plausibility, and therefore authority, of *Apostolicae Curae*. My own personal judgement is that with a fully traditional theology of ministry Anglican orders can and should in today's situation (though not necessarily so in that of the past) be accepted as 'valid' by the Catholic Church in the same way as it accepts the orders of Greeks, Copts and Ethiopians. This is a personal view but one which many Catholic theologians are coming to share. With less traditional theologies of ministry (at least less traditional for the Catholic West) it might be even easier to agree upon their 'validity'. But if all the same one accepts a hypothesis of strict invalidity as being at least too strong a possibility to ignore, what then? It is clear that today the Catholic Church, even where it refuses to recognize a valid ministry, does not refuse to recognize an efficacious ministry; it by no means considers the Anglican Eucharist to be a nothing. On the contrary it accepts such a Eucharist as the reverend, prayerful and fruitful memorial of the Lord, recalling his supper, death and resurrection in such a manner that God can and undoubtedly does use it as a main means of grace, as the sign which builds up the faith, mission, charity and sense of self-identity of the Christians participating in it. What Catholics gain in the Mass we must still recognize on such a hypothesis Anglicans may gain in their Mass, and in every explicit way they respond similarly. Can it be wrong for a Catholic to share for good reason with his fellow baptized in such a holy and orthodox prayer?

Let us remember that strictly we have faith in the 'valid' orders of no priest; there can always be some slight measure of human doubt. Our faith goes beyond the immediate occasion, in so far as the latter is particular, to that which is signified and intended to be signified in this way. We act upon the adequate convergence of probabilities and leave the rest to God. So, I would hold, is it now possible for Catholics to do in an Anglican eucharist on occasion. Yet increasingly, I suspect, a Catholic consensus will be found to admit the full acceptability of Anglican orders. So much here follows from the agreement on present belief when added to the unquestionably careful handing on of the episcopal/presbyteral ministry which has always characterized the Anglican communion. The more we realize that we do indeed believe the same about the eucharist, worship in the same way, and ordain our priests in the same way, the more unlikely it will seem to us that God could in some significant degree consider the Anglican celebration of Mass to be null, to have some subtle 'invalidity' secretly undermining its acceptability.

In such circumstances Catholics and Anglicans cannot, I maintain, be wholly bound to desist from practising their baptismal right to intercommunicate, entering in, when welcomed, to the Eucharist of each other's community. An ecclesiastical judgement of a century ago which is not claimed to have the authority to bind belief is not strong enough to do that in the absence of other decisive reasons.

Consequently I hold that our baptismal right to share communion stands today basically un-negated. Nevertheless if eucharistic communion between Anglicans and Catholics is by no means impossible—and in fact in its own way the Secretariat of Unity has already recognized the fact—it is still, when we consider our overall ecclesiastical position, highly anomalous. Our Churches are seriously divided, and while there does exist some genuine hierarchical co-operation, true hierarchical communion certainly does not. Hierarchical communion is the minister and guard of eucharistic communion, and it is anomalous to have the latter without the former (even if the latter be only intermittent and by way of exception), but it is also anomalous, as we have seen, and indeed still more profoundly anomalous to have and recognize a baptismal communion with no eucharistic communion. The greater the overall degree of communion, the less the degree of anomaly. If we cannot wholly remove the anomaly we can partially marginalize it, and that is what we are really in process of doing throughout the ecumenical movement as sharing grows and division diminishes. We have today continually to press the eastern analogy upon our western divisions. Pope Paul has declared that Rome and Constantinople are in 'almost full communion', although there is still no strict hierarchical communion between the two and Orthodox bishops did not participate in the Vatican Council. Communion can grow by degrees; that between Rome and Constantinople has certainly grown during the last ten years. Communion between Rome and Canterbury has done the same since the first visit of Archbishop Fisher to Pope John; it is still not as close today as the other, but there is no absolute reason why it should not grow almost imperceptibly to the same position. Such growth does, of course, require not only alteration in the relationship between the two communions but also in the character of each. As this process goes on, as our sense of common faith and practice of a shared community steadily increases, so do the intrinsic reasons which formerly made eucharistic intercommunion quite inappropriate come to fade away. Inevitably this is a somewhat confused process, just as our falling apart in the sixteenth century was, taking time and not affecting every place and person at the same moment.

Today we would seem to have reached the stage when a small but considerable minority upon each side is so aware of the implications of our common faith and so involved for one reason or another in common Christian life and mission that total non-intercommunion is becoming an impossible nonsense. Our serious spiritual need requires it and, as the Secretariat of Christian Unity has pointed out in its latest Instruction (June 1972) 'Spiritual need of the Eucharist is not merely a matter of personal spiritual growth: simultaneously, and inseparably, it concerns our entering more deeply into Christ's Church'.

The inherent logic of our common baptism and the eucharistic rights it bestows is taking over. I notice how regularly in many parts of Africa today Catholics and Anglicans taking part in common Church meetings share in the eucharist without hesitation upon any one's part. Fifteen years ago that could not have happened. There are growing areas of joint mission, common theological colleges, retreats, missions, ecumenical conferences, besides inter-church marriages and regions of ecclesiastical diaspora (in which one Church or the other lacks ministerial structures) in which today it would seem appropriate to share the eucharist together—but only, of course, when the participants themselves are convinced that it is right and proper. At present this will certainly not always be the case. Such a vast change of community attitudes as this cannot come all at once, but to bring it about at all some people are called to take a lead. We should be grateful to Bishop Elchinger of Strasburg because he has recently done so. Surely if any city has a special ecumenical vocation within Europe for the recovery of unity that city should be Strasbourg. In December 1972 in an instruction relating to mixed marriages he allowed non-Catholics in certain circumstances to be received to Catholic communion and Catholics to receive communion in another Church. This is certainly a step beyond anything the Secretariat of Unity has hitherto explicitly authorized, at least as regards the latter. The Secretariat has, however, more than once stressed that it is not for it but for local bishops to take the lead in this matter, deciding about particular pastoral situations; and it has accepted that mixed marriages are among those situations of serious spiritual need in which non-catholics may receive Catholic communion. It has recognized too that the spiritual need which is what the call for intercommunion is all about is not merely a matter of responding to a person's individual sacramental deprivation but of the necessity of 'entering more deeply into Christ's Church'. In responding to this need intercommunion can have a real ecclesial function. It is a growth point to be gently encouraged whereby our separated communions discover themselves again as effectively a single communion, the one communion which is the Church, achieving its renewed unity not basically through a juridical process but through the authentic celebration of the sacrament which makes the Church what she truly is: the body of Christ.

8

Liberalism

I am a liberal, and as one who claims the name, written with either a small or a large L, and to stand firm in the tradition of Charles James Fox, I want to say why I so identify myself and why I think the liberal tradition to be all in all by far the best thing in the world's modern political experience.

A liberal is one who asserts the primacy in importance in the political order of freedom—in the political order because in the human order. It is the greatest quality of man and it has been indeed the rallying cry of man in every age, his innate need. It is a quality which is not wholly loseable, yet a man can be more or less free, and so can societies. It is the mark of the liberal that he is committed to prizing freedom and to the enterprise of creating and recreating a political society which reflects this central quality of man. If he is a Christian he will either have discovered this sense of man and of society in scripture or, turning there, will find it mightily confirmed.

Our perennial political task is to evolve and sustain institutions for society which in given geographical, economic and cultural conditions provide a maximum of freedom for all the people within that society. The opposite to a liberal society is a tyrannical, oppressive society and the deliberate maintenance of tyranny or its extension I hold to be fascism. Such fascism can be and is found on both the so-called right and the so-called left. The fascism of Stalin and the fascism of Hitler are indeed finally not significantly different. It is the task of the liberal to challenge them both with all that is in him, while demonstrating the viability and immeasurable worth of concrete institutions which guard and reflect human freedom: law courts which operate out of the control of politicians and policemen; a press which can sharply criticise the government and disagree within itself; rival social and political organisations which reflect group interests but cannot coerce the commonwealth; peaceful processes whereby major laws can be changed and the highest rulers displaced.

No society has a perfect set of such institutions but some come a great deal nearer to it than others. It is the belief of the liberal that the central political struggle relates to coming nearer or departing further from such a pattern.

In the more intense and naive days of the cold war it was widely felt in the West that Stalinist tyranny was something wholly different in kind from any other tyranny and that the political leaders of the West, being opposed to Russia in the West-East power struggle of the time, must be equally opposed to the oppressive character of Russian government. We are able to distinguish things more clearly today. We can see that countries with very different systems of internal government can be joined in international alliance—as history has indeed shown time and again. We can see too that despite such different systems the temper of the governors may be disturbingly similar. When one remembers the secret black list of over two hundred American intellectuals and public figures produced by Nixon's aides—people who were to be watched and discredited by every possible means, one can guess that the same administration is not going to lose much sympathy over the plight of Sakharov or Solzhenitsyn. The Nixon-Brezhnev relationship was not only one of big power détente but of a certain common temper of government. To say this is not to equate the two situations. The objective structures of American society have a massive liberalism built into them, which may be tarnished but does still limit the fascist tendencies of government in a very notable way—that is indeed what the public process of Watergate has been all about. Such structures are almost entirely absent in the USSR where the individual has with immensely much greater heroism to stand up for freedom almost unsupported beyond the naked strength of his conscience.

Where such structures are absent—or absent for a notably large part of the population—the liberal is not in principle opposed to violent revolution, and he never has been. But where they at least partially exist, he prefers both for deep reasons of principle and for practical reasons to work within them, remembering how often violent revolution in fact breaks down society's barriers of restraint and produces a still greater oppressiveness than that of the preceding situation.

Where the true liberal of today must differ most considerably from that of the nineteenth century is that he will take a more economically sophisticated view of how the freedom of the majority is to be ensured. Political freedom is not meaningful in a laissez-faire system which has betrayed the majority of people to economic servitude. Marxist and socialist analysis forces us to rethink the control which is necessary over the economic pressures upon an authentically human society, but it should not affect our final criterion of freedom, nor the value we see in maintaining the sort of political structures for such freedom which the west has evolved over the centuries.

As a matter of fact orthodox Marxist theory by itself is not nearly sophisticated enough an instrument for the analysis of oppression in all its forms. But the Marxist is an ally when he is a liberal, he is an enemy when he is not—he is then a Fascist. Perhaps that is the soundest lesson we can learn from contemporary Russia or contemporary eastern Europe. A Marxist can be a liberal. Dubcek was, whatever he called himself, and it was because he valued so highly human freedom and the sort of institution and check which make freedom possible that he attempted what he did and fell as he did. Equally many a man and many a party calling themselves liberal are not so at all: they are little more than the soft glove of tyranny. That is only too clear in South Africa and it has given the name a tainted sound but such people are as different from the true and inherently relentless liberal tradition of the West as chalk is from cheese.

The road of liberalism is a narrow road: how obvious was the falling away in the soft line *The Times*, for instance, took at first towards the overthrow of Allende in comparison with its condemnation of that of Dubcek. Yet each is a clear example of a fascist victory over a government struggling for an essentially liberal view of society within an intensely difficult situation. But the liberal will not see the world as black and white. He knows that no country is fully free; that oppression, torture and police brutality can take place even within a country with such a strong liberal and legal tradition as the United Kingdom, yet he does not therefore equate the British system with the Albanian. Characteristic liberal institutions such as *Amnesty International* and the *Minority Rights Group* know that they have a task almost everywhere. The liberal does not refuse to give credit for genuine advances even in so unfree a country as the Soviet Union or South Africa, but he will beware of the soft handshake for the visiting parliamentarian or tourist offered by the torturer's public relations officer (a charming gentleman who once spent a year in Oxford).

If there is one man more than another who has fought the liberal fight in our time for all the world to see I believe that man to be Solzhenitsyn, though his own personal tone is undoubtedly entirely different from that which agnostic liberals in the West have tended to cultivate. Perhaps he is a liberal almost *malgré soi*, more probably he is it in the depths of his being just because authentic christianity can finally be no other. He has fought his fight against Stalinism with that final confidence in the freedom of the individual as against the massive mechanisms of society, which characterises the perennial liberal: 'I cannot accept that it is impossible to reverse the disastrous course of history, that one human soul with confidence in itself cannot influence the most powerful force on earth.'

9

Interfaith marriage and the wider society

A Midsummer Night's Dream is, perhaps, more than any other of Shakespeare's plays, a celebration of marriage—of marriage seen as a social as well as a personal covenant whether it be entered into for reasons of State or intense private love. The whole structure of the play suggests that marriage is of much more than personal interest; it is the public bonding at every level of society (as it is in *As You Like it*) of the two deeply distinct halves of the world. It is a social union replacing the skirmishing of the sexes manifest in war, in avoidance, in pursuit, in joking relationships. With Theseus and Hippolita's wedding war comes to an end; Oberon and Titania's reconciliation provides for the reuniting of the two halves of the elves. The loving and bedding of the wooing and wedding of Hermia and Helena are seen in this context to be but the tip of the iceberg (to use an inappropriate metaphor) as regards the full reality of marriage.

Marriage, in fact, is the inter-sex covenant, the social institution which brings together most closely and most deliberately in a relationship of communion and creative tension two such dissimilar partners as man and woman. It is better to marry than to fight, much better. But it does involve the sacrifice of much of that predominantly one sex society to which one has hitherto largely belonged; it draws the boy from his primary loyalty to football club or hunting companions, the girl from weaving or the typists' pool. Each, of course, has sallied out from those one-sex fellowships frequently enough, but now it is different—the balance of life is to change. The stag party expresses this change with a symbolically final celebration of the past. An alliance has been arranged—a covenant between two parties with their different attitudes, education, occupation. It is to be a bridge, establishing a new focal point of fellowship and loyalty, but one which does not eradicate earlier clusters of fellowship and loyalty upon either side; it will weave them together into a new pattern affecting a great many people within whose lives bride and groom already belong.

In the perennial tradition of Africa, Asia, and Europe too, marriage has been seen as an alliance, not just of two individuals, but of two families, two kin groups, at times even of two cities or kingdoms; today, often more significantly, of two friendship networks. The rules of incest, endogamy and exogamy are complex, varied and much disputed as to their full meaning and origin. Occasionally, and we shall come back to some instances of it, a society builds up firm rules of endogamy (marrying within one's group), but generally the primary concentration of custom was rather upon exogamy (marrying outside one's group). Incest is the greatest marital crime but far beyond the boundaries of incest are the prohibited degrees, the clan or village groups one must avoid. By a rule of exogamy one is driven out to create new relationships not only for oneself but for one's blood relatives, the whole society of one's kindred. One is allying the group with another group. Even today the arrival of a French daughter-in-law, for instance, is sure to affect a whole nest of people in their attitudes to another group of people if in fairly unformalised ways. Much history, social and political, can be written as a record of the consequences of marriage in the interweaving of traditions, the reshaping of loyalties, the expanding network of friendships, the creation of new responsibilities to offer support. In many an African society the affinal obligations consequent upon one's kin after marriage are precise, complex, recognised of right. Elsewhere such things may be more implicit, but they do not disappear. Indeed in certain historical cases, political marriages—as of a French or Spanish princess with an English king, as of Isabella with Ferdinand—express and bring about a politically altered relationship involving millions of people in the two societies somehow united by the marriage.

It is perfectly true that the danger here is for the personal relationship at the core of marriage to be veritably crushed by the political significance: the girl becomes but a pawn in the diplomacy or territorial aggregation of her father or bridegroom. And such was often the case. Yet it does not have to be so: social and personal significance are not antipathetic but complimentary; the social bonding possible through marriage is no substitute for the personal relationship. Separate either wholly from the other and you get a recipe for disaster: either the total politicisation or the total privatisation of marriage negates the deep sense of the covenant which is, even naturally, *sacramentum*. The social and political dimension must grow out from the personal bond—

sometimes almost technically, more often by its symbolism and the further opportunities for new social links doubly weighted that this particular household, constituted in the way it has been, now affords. Thus, to take once more a royal and large scale example, Albert and Victoria did, in their union, both symbolise and stimulate the Anglo-German understanding of the mid-nineteenth century.

All this points to the inherent social function of marriage as something which makes a person face out of his or her own society to achieve the deepest relationship in life with someone until now of a different society, in order that subsequently they will not only be themselves joined together, while still belonging to a greater or lesser extent to each former group, but their union will affect the social horizons and obligations of many other members of each society as well. These consequences are not the odd and almost regrettable accidents of marriage, but form a large part of its central purpose; they are consequences of which most societies stand from one point of view or another in serious need if they are not to become ghettos of blood, culture, class or creed.

Such is the challenge of marriage as a public reality, a challenge it has to meet in appropriate form in many a different social milieu. It is quite true that society in the past was structured in most places very much more by marriage and kinship than it is today; marriage today has a relatively secondary role to play in the shaping of society; indeed the consequent over-personal-isation of marriage (and the theoretical justification for this provided in works such as those of Fr Schillebeeckx) can be part of the whole modern problem. Nevertheless the social role of marriage today is not nearly so slight as many might assume. A very considerable portion of one's leisure activities, enduring personal relationships outside the household, social responsibilities, letter writing are related to the wider family; and then there is the whole pattern of one's non-related friends depending upon the character and loyalties of the two people who first make up the family. That character and those loyalties may be such as to cut across significant frontiers or, on the contrary, to remain entirely inside them. In any society which includes such frontiers it will be dangerous if almost all the marriages fail to leap the frontier and remain instead endogamous in regard to the issue which is here precisely the significant divide; it may be a class divide, an international divide, a racial divide, or a religious divide. It will be still more dangerous if endogamy of such a sort be erected into a moral obligation.

The essential pattern is always much the same. Two groups

of people with decided differences are living side by side and in considerable contact. Without some genuinely close personal relationships and the achievement of at least a measure of institutionalised solidarity misunderstanding and tension are inevitable, open conflict probable. The situation calls for friendship and the weaving of a network of relationships; if this be allowed, alliances will follow, inter-society marriages providing the sacramental expression of that human fellowship now admitted between the two groups as in the reconciliation song from *Oklahoma*:

> Cowboys dance with the farmers' daughters
> Farmers dance with the ranchers' gals.

But inevitably inter-society marriage will threaten the purity of the tradition, the identity of either group. And so groups frequently frown at such marriages or ban them entirely, and as soon as they do so the openness proper to a human society faced with other societies has to be replaced by the sense of the *lager*, the besieged citadel: the purity of race or faith is held to be in danger. They go endogamous. The blue blooded must not marry the peasant; a Hapsburg may finally find himself unable to marry anyone but another Hapsburg; Montague must not marry Capulet; nor white black; Catholic must not marry Protestant; nor Christian non-Christian.

The tendency here is, first, to exclude large blocks of our neighbours from the possibility of being a group with whom it is possible to make a covenant alliance, and secondly, if someone slips through the net, then to insist that a person marrying from another group must wholly enter into one's own. Marriage is acceptable only with a prior 'conversion' which—if complete—is really to deny the nature of the covenant. In true marriage the unity of the bride and bridegroom does not exclude a continuing relationship with either side, though understandably one or other will frequently be the dominant one. To which kin will the children chiefly belong? In a patrilineal system we get one answer, in a matrilineal one another. It is interesting to see how in Africa, where there are inter-church marriages, the religion of the children tends to be settled by the kinship pattern of the tribe: in a patrilineal society they will follow the religion of the father, in a matrilineal society the church of the mother.

There are patrilineal marriage patterns in Africa where the bride actually enters the clan of the husband, but far more frequently she remains in her own. While the children take their father's clan, they will still have particular obligations—a special relationship—to their mother's clan. This suggests that a mixed marriage too can indeed be structured in a number of ways; and it is clear from experience that this is so. One cannot insist that there be no 'conversion'; to some extent, at least, there should indeed be one upon either side: a quite new approach to and communion with the society represented by one's partner and the values it cherishes. On the other hand if one side insists that there be a quasi-total conversion, then the marriage loses its function as a social covenant. It becomes not a bridge but a new cause for antipathy and division. And this, alas, is what civil and church authority has at times made of it. There has been the endeavour to nullify its bridging power by the inequality of terms on which the two partners enter it in relation to their former status. As a consequence Jessica's alliance with Lorenzo can only be one more item in the alienation of Shylock. Bob Williamson in the song marries Bridget McGinn but 'turns papist' and consequently has to 'flee to the province of Connaught' from his native Ulster. If somehow he hadn't had to flee, been allowed to remain orange and Bridget papist, then perhaps there might have been no bullets of the Provos and the UVF. If two groups live cheek by jowl and there is no marriage, then there will be war.

Of course, even though the individual, wife or husband, does enter the clan, church or political allegiance of the other partner, he or she has still a whole family behind him whose proper links with the new generation are intended to assert the under-valued side. The role of grandparents is an important one and, while it is understandable, it is mistaken for parents to resent the bond between children and grandparents. This and the multiplicity of other relationships with uncles, aunts and cousins are the particular links which make real the wider implications of the social covenant of marriage—links which in any 'mixed' situation weave back and forward across the borders of faith, class or race.

Clearly there are limits to the ability of a marriage to be a bridge without disaster; this depends both upon the capacity of the partners and the willingness of the two societies to be so linked. The hostility of Montague and Capulet was such that the attempt to unite them came to immediate disaster, though in doing so it pricked the whole absurd bubble of their hostility. The incompatibility of the two was annulled in death. Some societies are murderously opposed to mixing; others will simply stone-wall. But the capacity of two people to bridge the divide can only be discovered in the trying, and it should be allowed to do it in its own way, though of course people may rightly be warned of the difficulties. The basic principle remains that true human unity is never a unity of uniformity.

Human communion is always the bonding of the diverse. But how far in a single household can the diverse be acceptable, even tolerable? What is possible for some, will appear quite impossible for others. There must clearly exist some deep sharing of conviction, beyond any division of loyalties, but such a sharing is quite achievable across many divides. One must always start from the position that marriage does not and should not end previous loyalties, though it may materially alter them. A husband in taking on commitments to his wife does not withdraw from those he already has to parents, sisters and others. These commitments will then be shared; but others, more elusive or spiritual, will remain the possession of one alone, though respected by the other. A degree of cultural, political or religious division within the household which would be intolerable for some, is in fact found acceptable, and even stimulating, by others. In reality one does not have a single model for 'the' perfect marriage; and marriages, anyway, are all imperfect: over the years achieving more or less according to one or another model. It may seem to some ideally desirable that a husband and wife should agree upon all fundamental matters, and with some people and in some societies that may appear easy enough. But in the world as a whole, and in many parts of it, there is no such agreement, and it is both unreal and undesirable to require it for marriage. On the contrary, it is socially dangerous, as has been suggested above, to have such divisions in society, and not to have them also within marriage: not to allow marriage to cross them. It is in marriage indeed that they can be challenged, overcome in a deeper unity, but only through accepting the possibility of continued tension and disagreement.

One obvious and common example in modern western society is marriage between the Christian and the 'modern pagan'. It does in fact frequently work out very happily; it would be highly undesirable socially if it did not exist; and yet the basic religious gap here may be immense—far wider than between two Christians of different churches or between a Christian and an African adhering to a traditional religion or a Christian and a Muslim.

People are often only very inadequately aware of their predicament in this area or others; they are within a social situation which they have not analysed and do not very closely foresee the pressures it will exert on them, the demands it will make. As time goes on they may respond in a positive manner, they may survive for ever largely uncomprehending, or they may be overwhelmed. This woman has married this man: they love one another. In fact a cluster of circumstances, attractions, preferences, the leap of personal trust, all this has brought them together. They need one another and want to put this relationship in some way first, but seldom (and then somewhat unnaturally) intend to abandon the vast network of relationships and loyalties already woven into their lives. Yet one is a Christian, the other an animist, a Muslim, a modern non-believer. Probably neither is consciously prepared for the intensely difficult task of growing into a deep personal union with someone with whom much of what is deep in one's own life cannot just like that be shared. But such is the nature of life, and marriages do in fact achieve different sorts of harmony and co-operation; they can succeed in different ways, while some can fail—wholly or partly. Many do fail, and for a variety of reasons. Yet seldom, probably, chiefly for this one. One may be more tolerant of religion than of many other things in the close quarters of a single household. The great majority of inter-something marriages are doubtless not lived with a great degree of deliberate vocation and self-analysis. They may not bridge the chasm theoretically, yet many do so in practice and in doing so may yet a little diminish the theoretical separation. Between a believing Christian and someone of another faith, there can in fact be much in common at the level of personal religion: faith in God, in providence, in goodness, in the need to forgive, in the obligation of loyalty, in the acceptance of the true. These are the things decisive in anyone's life and they can cross the widest theoretical divides of religion. It can well happen that a Christian and a non-Christian are more closely linked at the level of the deep things of religion than, say, a practising and a lapsed Catholic.

Many such unions which do in fact exist the Church, alas, has refused canonically to recognise. But many others it has recognised, more easily in earlier centuries, more marginally in later times. From one such Augustine was born, though admittedly his subsequent rather negative view of marriage does not speak particularly in its favour. Today there are thousands of Christians in Africa, at least, who do live in an inter-faith marriage recognised by the church, for they married before they were baptised, though they may well already have been catechumens. The pattern of a Christian wife and a non-Christian husband is a common one, not only in Africa but elsewhere too, notably Japan. Doubtless in its tidy and canonical way the modern Church has not much liked such arrangements but equally it has to a large extent accepted them, recognising (despite clerical reluctance) that the world largely makes itself, that marriage is—first of all—a natural fact which one has to live with in all its jagged splendour rather than construct on *a priori* lines.

The duty of the wise man, the understanding legislator or pastor or parents in State or Church, is not to outlaw the outlandish marriage, to fling out boy or girl because he or she has married beyond the frontier, but rather to celebrate the event while endeavouring to provide in an unostentatious way the additional support of which anyone in a somewhat exposed position may stand in need. One should acknowledge that this is marriage at its most meaningful, its most sublime, and that some people at least must be called in this way even if—as normally happens in human experience—they have themselves not perceived half the significance of that to which they have personally set themselves. A society in which this is absolutely not acceptable is sure to be a society in a bad way psychologically. For here indeed marriage is being most true to itself, God's chosen instrument within man's own order for social reconciliation, made in Christ into sacrament of the final reconciling covenant. If its nature, in all its personal and fleshly particularity, is to signify the intensely improbable marriage alliance of infinite God and a finite people, it will do so authentically the more it really is an alliance between the unlike, unlike in spirit, unlike in flesh, drawing the diverse into an authentic unity. Nothing is more truly sacrament than a loving, persevering marriage covenant which crosses the bounds of faith or race. This is rather the ideal of human and Christian marriage than the *Catholic Fireside* union of boy and girl from the same parish, the same street, the same sodality: as a model of marriage the latter may appear to border on the incestuous.

Of course marriages vary, as do ministries. The rich diversity of purpose within this one institution cannot be fully realised in the particular instance. In hard fact it is perfectly acceptable that some be more endogamous, some more exogamous; and their characteristic life styles, their mode of relating the household fellowship to wider society, the virtues they most noticeably substantiate, will vary accordingly. Within the complexity of human nature and of modern society, one certainly does not want to declare one pattern normative.

All I wish to suggest here is that the 'traditional' Catholic concentration upon the importance of avoiding a religiously 'mixed' marriage, or at the least controlling and next to nullifying its bridging capacity, implies a restrictive and inadequate understanding of the very nature of marriage, both socially and theologically. Adherence to religion and the state of marriage are alike social realities; and that side of the social purpose of marriage which can be covered by the word 'alliance' (relating to a wider group of people than bride and groom) is as relevant for a religiously divided society as for one divided according to any other criteria.

There is no gap in human society which cannot be bridged in marriage or which, in principle, should not be bridged. Such is the nature of mankind. We must affirm most emphatically that it is and should be an inter-marrying society. To the extent that we exclude inter-marriage we exclude the full recognition of our common humanity, and we deny too the adequate sacramentality of marriage itself: we would be admitting that its covenant power has inherent limitations, and that it is not, even with the added grace of Christian faith, up to being an appropriate sign of ultimate reconciliation. We must not accept that. Marriage is always difficult and dangerous. No man or woman can commit him or herself inter-personally and inter-sexually to the extent that marriage demands without difficulty and danger. Covenants always cross frontiers and all frontiers are perilous. But if the Church of Christ is committed to working in truth within the hard realities of social fact and human division for the realisation of a communion, a *koinonia*, of mankind, and has two blessed instruments to bring about and symbolise such communion: the eucharist covenant and that marriage covenant which she did not make and which did not begin in Christ's life but has been with us always 'from the beginning', then she must welcome and use these where and as they are, not imposing limits at odds with their meaning. Where division is deepest, there the pioneer is most needed to step out: to establish that inter-personal covenant which yet somehow draws the kindred with him. Leaping the sex barrier, he will leap too that of class, of race, of religion. Instead of excommunicating the mixer, it is surely the role of the Church to bless the pioneer who thus steps out to extend the frontiers of fellowship.

10

Called to liberate:
mission and South Africa

'You my friends, were called to freedom' (Galatians 5: 13)

How do we proclaim a gospel of freedom? That is today's essential missionary question. Let us not doubt that the Church not only has had, but still has, a missionary task; indeed, that this missionary task is so fundamental and primary for the Church's very being and *raison d'etre* that without it the Church cannot justifiably be. It had the unlimitable mission and explosive power of Jesus the new Adam and the Spirit of God in its very charter of origin. The church has been called into being by the gospel of God made manifest in and by Jesus Christ. By baptism and continuing faith its members identify themselves with that Gospel in all its liberating power. They receive for themselves an initiating liberation—entry on principle into the sphere of God's freedom demonstrated in Christ—and have then throughout their lives both to digest that freedom existentially across the complexity of psychological and social experience and to communicate it, in so far as they are able, to others.

If the Gospel is true at all, it is both important and universal—universally important. By definition it is not a geographically, culturally, racially or sexually limited thing, but a geographically, culturally, racially and sexually transcending thing. It is a message from Adam to Adam. If it is not received by the whole human race, something must be—in terms of the Gospel—greatly amiss, and satisfaction with such a situation in principle is intrinsically a denial of the meaning of the Gospel and must negate the consistent Christian position of someone entertaining such satisfaction.

Moreover, while we believe it to be of the nature of the grace of Christ to be at work immensely effectively far beyond the limits of those explicitly conscious of that grace or willing to interpret the human condition and themselves in gospel terms of any sort, yet it is also of the nature of the Gospel of that grace to be an explicit message and to impose an obligation upon its receivers not only themselves to recognise the universal power of God's grace at work in all human situations, but also to strive to further the confessing acceptance of such a gospel by others that they may respond consciously, as befits a man, to this most significant aspect of their condition.

Yet the majority of this world today do not accept the Christian Gospel. They do not interpret their condition in Christian terms. Hence the missionary task of the Church is not and cannot be over. To suggest that altered political and cultural conditions have somehow brought it to an end would be a wholly unacceptable, and gospelly destructive, form of revisionism. To suggest, on the other hand, that those altered conditions can radically change the structures, pattern of presentation, geographical priorities of mission should be to state the obvious. If the frontier between belief and disbelief runs down the middle of my heart, then here and foremost here the believing half must plead with, must strive with reason human and divine to satisfy the troubled agnosticism of the unbelieving half.

In the heart the task may start, and here too it finds its term; yet of itself it is a public thing. What we need to ask, as it has very seldom been asked, is how we have to conceive the shape of a proper public proclamation of the Gospel. It is, I hope, self-evidently, not the proclamation of a non-implicating corpus of information, but a way of life. If, then, the message is to be proclaimed credibly, it must surely be proclaimed in such a way that the bearer's own life is congruous with it, constituting a persuasive and not a dissuasive. If one's message be no more than 'twice two is four', I take it that the credibility of the message will not be greatly affected by any outside behaviour of its bearer, though even here an excess of cruelty in the teacher might so incense his hearers as to reject anything whatsoever coming from him.

If, however, your message is of its nature something not self-evident, something pervasive of life, something which if true should be decisively significant for the pattern of behaviour of those accepting it, then, if the message be proclaimed with all orthodox precision but by a person behaving in a notably and noticeable manner such as to be or appear contradictory to the message, then that manner must necessarily undermine the force of the verbal content of the proclamation and indeed as a complex whole either act powerfully as a counter-persuasive to its reception or bring about the communication of a seriously defective message. If one tortures people on weekdays, or justifies or condones their torture, or regularly drinks one's beer with the torturers, and then proclaims a gospel of love in ever so pure a manner on Sundays, then the behaviour of the weekday will either act as strong preventative from the acceptance of the Sunday message or result in the Sunday message being accepted in a decisively distorted form.

It is well to remind ourselves that while in our various churches and missions we speak of the one God, name the same name of Jesus Christ, quote biblical texts from this book or that, yet it can be that effectively we do not necessarily thereby preach the same God or the same Christ. Nominally we may have a common Gospel; practically by a process of selecting a certain pattern of texts for use, stressing different doctrines or attributes of God, we may proclaim very different, even contradictory Gospels—even in their explicitly mouthed thrust. Still more so when the proclaimed Gospel is seen as being effectively constituted by the complex whole of the messenger's behaviour and life style. What is received may then be different indeed from what the latter would think he has been saying.

There may be societies in which the playing of golf can be properly regarded as a non-significant recreation. But this is certainly not true in many other places, where it is on the contrary a markedly elitist recreation which very publicly links its devotees with an over-privileged class or racial minority group. The golf club itself may have a colour or financially decisive in-built class bar. To play golf here is to say something important about this society; it is freely for one's personal pleasure to assert one's fellowship, even friendship, with one group of people, one's deliberate segregation from others. A choice of partner on the golf course can carry with it further socio-political implications; if one is professedly a Christian missionary it can carry socio-political-ecclesial implications. One is in a subtle, but for those watching from an excluded group, very real way identifying with another person; if that other person is known as a payer of very inadequate wages, or one who will not allow a black man to enter his house through his front door, then by playing golf with him one may be effectively identifying with such behaviour, or at the very least asserting it to be non-significant. The message of the golf course may be a more compelling message than that of the pulpit because it is—with great probability—a more personally revealing one. The professionalism of the pulpit carries with it a necessarily considerable discount in sincerity.

The point here is that the congruity required in the Gospel

bearer's life style is not just a matter of personal morals and manners; it has to go right through the social, political and cultural presuppositions built into a personal life style, and that is indeed to say a good deal. Since every Gospel bearer is a sinner and no one can eliminate all the structural pressures of an unjust society from the shaping of his own life, at least unless one flees to the desert, some degree of incongruity has not only to be tolerated but is quite inevitable. But when the incongruity is accepted as part of the ecclesial or missionary system and relates to that which is precisely what the Gospel should here primarily be challenging, then indeed the incongruity can become quite intolerable.

The little Sisters of Jesus do not preach at all, yet they witness all the time—on buses (they are, I believe, the only white people in South Africa who manage to travel on African buses), at work, in the open fellowship of their home. In fact we all witness in one direction or another—all behaviour is inclusive of a message, generally, doubtless, a rather weak message, sometimes a very strong one; we preach across our relationship with a TV set, our relationship to our books, through conversation at dinner. By a tone of voice we draw people into something, cast them out, proclaim patterns of propriety. What the Little Sisters say to us, without of course ever being so bold as to put it into words, is that this sort of witness can be so much more important than the formal exercises, so much more persuasive and fruitful, that it is worth giving up the latter entirely if we can only get the former right. If we offer both, but the two messages be at variance—not the variance of forgetfulness, impatience, sudden irritation—but the variance involved in a steady pattern of significant behaviour—then we may be becoming, not a sign of salvation, but a countersign, an almost subliminal but psychologically decisive barrier to the communication of the Gospel.

It is not possible to attempt here the analysis of a typology of Gospels, offered today and in the past, nor to outline and justify criteria for preferring one to another. I can only state rather simply my own conviction as to what the true Gospel should centrally consist in, so that major violation of this central theme is to be emphatically judged evangelically counter-productive. The Gospel affirms that the service of the living God, utterly incumbent upon man, is to be found primarily not in the keeping of the Sabbath or the worship of the temple but in the doing of justice to one's fellowmen, one's neighbour. Justice is the only finally fit worship for Yahweh and justice in this full Christian sense involves liberation—freeing one's neighbour from the inhuman pressures to which he is subjected; from the cup of cold water offered at the moment of thirst onwards.

The Christian Gospel proclaims the priority of justice and the service of others, in and through the life, death and resurrection of Jesus, in whom we discover at once the will of God, the power to do it, the consciousness that we have not done so, the gift of forgiveness for not having done so. Receiving this Gospel, this *kerygma*, it compels us to undertake secular human service, *diakonia*, and to enter into fellowship, *koinonia*. Just as in life Jesus expressed and embodied his mission through three integrally inter-involved channels; the friendship and fellowship of his company, *koinonia*; the message he proclaimed, the *kerygma* of his word; the service to those in affliction he continually gave, the *diakonia* of response to immediate human need. Across these three inextricably interwoven strands he both incarnated and pointed to the reality, the sufficiency, the superabundance, the invincibility of divine love.

The Christian kerygma is so intrinsically diakonal and koinonial, that pure and orthodox as it might verbally appear, it is impure and unorthodox if it be not koinonially and diakonally integrated; the word of God and the freedom of God incarnate in a place, a time, a pattern of words and of behaviour. Segregate your eucharist racially, exclude inter-racial koinonia, and it becomes impossible to celebrate the eucharist in a kerygmatically true way. The word of God, the message of ultimate liberation can only be entered into through this glass of water, this challenge to a corrupt tyranny, this gesture of reconciliation, this endeavour of immediate liberation from the burden of oppression. 'You fed me, you visited me in prison, enter into the kingdom.' Nowhere else is the gate of heaven.

If such be the Gospel then its missionary bearer cannot offer an authentic message of divine liberation unless he concretise it through the immediate *diakonia*, the here and now liberation from oppression, a tangible entering into freedom across which we can somehow already experience the expanding corridors of an eternal freedom. My friends, we have been called to freedom, the freedom of God, to bask in it, to proclaim it, to share it; to somehow incarnate it in the sphere around us, as we have to incarnate the truth, the mercy, the love of God; create life styles, structures of society which—while never adequately succeeding—yet with deep seriousness attempt here and now some image, some helpful pointer towards, some token of conviction that these things of God really are and by us are believed to be. We affirm the freedom of God bestowed upon us by committing ourselves to liberation, to the cause of that human freedom, which incorporates justice and love and which, in both the experience and the mythology of man, has ever been our dearest quality, our most unabandonable cause, our nearest point to deity.

The Gospel of freedom is a commission to liberate, to challenge hunger, injustice, the exploitation of man by man, in the name of the living God. That is mission. And it is centrally violated if the verbal message of ultimate liberation be detached from its matrix of temporal liberation (which is always a mixed up physical, psychological, social, political, economic business) and be offered instead as a 'pure', almost non-temporal message. Such a message is one of a number of pseudo-gospels, and we always have pseudo-gospels among us. To avoid being enmeshed by them we have to consider not only the theology but the solid structures of our mission very hard indeed in relationship with a given situation. To proclaim the Gospel cannot be done with political naivety, unless indeed it be the political naivety of the very poor. They may do so (and that maybe is how the early church got away with it) but the middle and upper classes cannot, and in a world context almost everybody in Britain today must be so classed.

Let us consider some examples. In proposing them, I wish to direct your attention to Southern Africa. It is an obviously relevant area for our discussion because as a matter of fact, it is still today one of the chief receiving areas in the world for western missionaries. David Livingstone already criticised the tendency of missionaries to huddle together in South Africa in the 1840s and it could be argued that, despite his criticism, this pattern never greatly diminished and is still very much with us today. It may have something to do with the climate.

Yet the alternative Livingstone proposed is also not beyond criticism. He too once came to Cambridge, to the Senate House, 'to direct your attention to Africa'. I go back to Africa, he said, 'to make an open path for commerce and Christianity'. Now it would be naive to condemn outright such a call linking commerce and Christianity. It is in the nature of things that the trader goes ahead and surely he may carry his faith with him. This conforms to a historic pattern of Christian advance in many ages and places. If the trader is a small man, his commerce may well provide a fairly suitable secular support for evangelical outreach; but in the context of the nineteenth-century Western expansionist capitalism and imperial domination often working through trade companies, the linking of commerce with Christianity could mean something very different.

It calls to mind the curious history of Magomero, Livingstone's chosen site for a mission in the Shire highlands. It was here that on his advice the Anglican UMCA missionaries, led by the venerable Bishop Mackenzie, established themselves. Mackenzie quickly died and his missionaries were withdrawn. Some time later the other side of Livingstone's dream took over; Magomero became instead an extensive coffee and cotton estate owned by none other than Livingstone's own son-in-law, Alexander Bruce, and later his grandson, Livingstone Bruce. The development of this vast European estate made its own contribution in the following years to the African land shortage and so to the unrest which culminated in the 1915 uprising. In that rising William Livingstone, the manager of the Bruce estates and cousin of David's, was beheaded at Magomero by that strange man, the Reverend John Chilembwe, leader of the revolt, a primal hero both of African independent Christianity and of nationalism. Thus full circle was reached within Livingstone's missionary strategy where mission had been planned to advance hand in hand with commerce and settlement in the circumstances of Southern Africa. Mackenzie's grave by the Shire river symbolises the western myth of its missionary approach; the graves of William Livingstone and John Chilembwe express another less happy side of the reality.

In Mozambique these last years we in the Catholic Church have at last begun to see what it all means; late, very late, yet better late than never. We have learnt what it can mean when Christian mission be officially declared, as in Portugal's Colonial Act of 1930, establishing the Salazarist system of the next 45 years, as 'instruments of civilisation and national influence' or, as in the Missionary Statute of 1941 which enacted in Portuguese legal form the agreement of the preceding year's Concordat, an 'institution of imperial utility', and when such a definition be in fact accepted by the Church through her agreement to work according to the terms of that statute and to accept the financial benefits and continual governmental control there laid down.

In *The Poor Christ of Bomba*, a work by the Cameroonian novelist, Mongo Beti, published in 1956, Drumont, a missionary, decides to leave the Cameroons; 'There are only two things I can do now', he says to the colonial official, 'I can stay in this country along with you, associated with you, and thus assist you to colonize it, with dreadful consequences; softening up the country ahead of you, and protecting your rear—for that's how you envisage our role, isn't it? Or else I can truly Christianize the country; in which case I'd better keep out of the way as long as you're still here.'

Soften the natives up in advance and then protect the imperial-ists' rear—this describes not inappropriately, not the intention of most missionaries, not the abstracted religious kernel of their teaching, but the over-all socio-political character of their work in a situation of oppressive imperialist or white racialist rule where the Christian missionary is linked by his own skin colour, national origin, style of life, and administrative network of church-state relationships with that oppressor.

The brutal clarity of that link in Portuguese Africa, spelt out in legal documents and read against the ever more harrowing background of the liberation struggle and consequent repression, finally drove the White Fathers in 1971 to come on principle to the decision of Beti's missionary of fifteen years before. System-atically used as instruments for the perpetuation of an oppressive regime, they had been condemned, not merely by the state but by Rome and by the bishops to an evangelically contradictory and personally disgraceful ambiguity. They withdrew—to the consternation of their superiors in both church and state. Since then many other missionaries in Mozambique have done the same, demanding a freedom which those superiors denied them.

In the revolt against the Concordat, we may be grateful for the existence of a concordat to drive missionaries to revolt, to make an affirmation against an exploitation of mission, an ambiguity in mission, which has not been limited to the Catholic Church or to Portuguese Africa. Nowhere were Catholic missionaries more free than in Mozambique to baptise, give all the sacraments, verbally preach an other-worldly Gospel; and nowhere has authen-tic missionary work become more impossible. By a withdrawal, a refusal to preach or baptise any more, they have preached and witnessed to the whole Gospel and borne the persona of the Church 'sacrament of salvation' far more truly than by remaining to verbalise the Gospel within an institutional pattern of work where by mere presence under the terms of the Concordat and its rel-ated documents, they were effectively not messengers of liberation but accomplices of oppression.

In South Africa there is no concordat, and on the surface most of the churches other than the Dutch Reformed are in some un-ease in relation to the government. Nevertheless, in practice there is the closest linking of all the white-ruled churches with the most deliberately and legally spelt out regime of oppression on the face of this earth. Despite the occasional statements of protest, the mainline churches in their leadership and ministry effectively adopt the life style of apartheid society. Having done so, their very existence with their religio-moral claims and sanctions, not only receive but reinforce that pattern. They soften up in advance, they protect in the rear. Their bishops, while theoretically serving a predominantly black community, have their homes in the most affluent white areas where black people can hardly come. They make daily use of facilities provided for 'whites only', and by their presence occupy posts which would otherwise be held by blacks.

Here indeed is the most basic point. Radical oppression in South Africa can only be maintained while white people are there in sufficient, indeed in increasing numbers. The fewer white people, the less the immigration, the more black people must be promoted, the more the structures of apartheid will crumble. It is for this reason that there has been an increasingly strong, and certainly well founded, call to halt white immigration into South Africa; a call coming from the World Council of Churches and other bodies. As Canon ffrench-Beytagh has remarked, 'I want to bring home to people in Britain that if you are an English artisan, you do harm simply by the fact of going to South Africa.' An English artisan but also an English priest. What is curious is that while the churches and missionary societies increasingly recognise the truth of the argument as regards other people, they remain most reluctant to apply it to themselves. Yet it is very hard to see how church work comes into a different category, or that the church has the moral right to appeal to others not to go to South Africa when it continues to send people there itself. For few white priests or other missionaries from abroad could it be seriously claimed that they have done other than effectively participate in the over-all pattern of discrimination; and for them so to do is more serious than for any other group of people in that it is intrinsically destructive of their professional task. A white missionary's apparently unprotesting presence within South Africa's racialist society is itself a strengthening of oppression and consequently *per se* evangelically counter-productive.

Moreover, why should it be necessary? There is a far higher proportion of church-going people in South Africa than in Britain. There are plenty of people there able and anxious enough to preach the gospel, to administer the sacraments, to exercise pastoral care, though doubtless to the extent that the structures of a church have been geared for decades to be administered by white people, largely expatriates, local people here and now do not, will not, almost cannot come forward.

I would suggest that only in two cases can the sending of white missionaries to Southern Africa be regarded today as so worthwhile in the particular instance that it is possible to see it as not participating in the general oppressive character of white immigration, and contributing therefore to a counter-witness to the Gospel. The first is when the individual missionary is profoundly committed to and adequately prepared for the task of bearing an effective and manifest counter-witness to that very oppression which would otherwise swallow up his very ministry within it. Of few people can this be true, or has it been true. Of some, thanks be to God, it surely is. David Russell, the Little Sisters of Jesus, Cosmos Desmond, Affonso Valverde and Martin Hernandez. The second is when someone is needed for a very skilled ministry of secular service which most certainly will not be provided by a local person. This could apply to a doctor sent to a Bantustan hospital and to some others; very seldom priests.

It is just because we remain absolutely committed to the preaching of the Gospel, the whole Gospel, that it is not open to us to send conventional white missionaries to South Africa. 'Woe to me if I do not evangelise.' That meant for the White Fathers: leave Mozambique. That, when we grasp the wholeness of the diakonal and koinonial kerygma of freedom, means: 'Do not go, white man, to South Africa. Do not go, white priest. The Gospel will not be wounded in South Africa at the present juncture by your absence, it will be by your presence.'

To decide not to go or to leave is, certainly, itself only a first step in the implementation of a programme of preaching the gospel of freedom, and a negative one. Liberation cannot be left there; new patterns of proclaiming that Gospel are being sought, must be found and may prove very costly. But what is necessary first is for the missionary movement to recognise that the degree of ambiguity which has entered into its work *viz à viz* liberation and oppression has reached an intolerable level. It can happen and has happened in the course of Church history that structures sincerely devised to realise some very worth while purpose come across the years, through their subtle reshaping by the less admirable pressures of this world, to be corrupted to such an extent that a renewed fidelity to the Gospel requires precisely their rejection. Such would seem here to be the case.

We are called in Christ to be free and share our freedom, to be liberated and to liberate; to enter into freedom at its deepest and most spiritual, to manifest what it means to have moved from Pauline 'slavery' to Pauline freedom in every dimension of the human life style. To assert, far more by the totality of our behaviour than by any single sermon, our obedient adherence to a gospel of freedom which, grounded in Exodus, proclaimed in

Jesus' Lucan programme in the Nazareth synagogue, can thrust down the mighty, raise up the lowly, be a trumpet blast to the ends of the earth which will challenge the towers of Satan, the dividing walls of apartheid, all the prisons of this world from Siberia to Robben Island.

In the words of the Battle Hymn of the Republic:

'As he died to make men holy,
Let us live to make them free'.

But indeed he himself died to make us free, and that is why we must both live and die to proclaim not only holiness but freedom. In our freedom is our likeness to God, our holiness. Never must we proclaim or can we proclaim a Gospel of holiness which is not too a Gospel of liberation. Remember you were called to freedom.

11

The reform of the ministry

Over the last decade there has been a not inconsiderable degree of reform within the ministry of the Catholic Church coupled with a steadily growing crisis in the priesthood. It would be a very grave miscalculation indeed to hold that this crisis will just fade away or that some slight increase in the number of young men in one country or another entering the seminary is indication that the worst is now over. The number of priests in the world is steadily declining. This is not a bad thing. In some places there were rather obviously too many, if in others (and much wider areas) there was already an equally obvious shortage. The decline in numbers is the inevitable concomitant of a vast process of declericalization which constitutes the most important structural change within the church of our time. As priests fade away the laity comes forward. Faced with the inadequacy of the one and the competence of the other, Church authority has pragmatically and at times reluctantly already sanctioned piece-meal a massive passing across to the non-ordained, lay and nuns, of tasks formerly reserved to the clergy.

It is now impossible for this process to cease or to be reversed and it is clear as day that for many such tasks there are lay people far better prepared than are the general body of clergy. Area after area of pastoral care and counselling is being taken over, as well as the greater part of the educational work within schools formerly carried out by priests, a large share of the general business of producing a contemporary theological literature, as also much ecclesiastical administration. Faced with this takeover, necessitated not only by the dwindling number of priests but also by their manifest overall inability to cope in today's world with the range of tasks formerly expected of them—despite so many years of training—faced too with an almost universal failure of episcopal leadership to help the clergy imaginatively to come through this long period of crisis, it is less than surprising if the numbers and morale of priests have seriously declined.

The crisis in the priesthood is not, however, only caused by decline; it is also caused by growth—both the growth in awareness of the possible scope of priestly ministry, the vast range of needs to be met and being met by some outstanding pioneers in many countries; and the growth in the sheer number of Church members in South America, Africa and some parts of Asia. In nearly every case the tradition of the celibate Catholic priesthood had really not taken root in those continents (India being the chief exception), and the number of local priests was extremely small in relation to the size of the church, alike in Chile, in the Philippines and in Zaire. The Church in these and many other countries has been run for generations by foreign priests and nuns from Western Europe and North America. Today that foreign clergy is diminishing and the sources of its recruitment have almost wholly dried up, while the worldwide cultural revolution of the post-colonial era have made that precise type of inter-continental structuring of the Church profoundly unsuitable; at the same time the population of the Southern continents is rising by leaps and bounds. If in a few countries (such as Nigeria and Tanzania) there has been some significant increase in the number of local priests, that increase remains woefully inadequate to prevent a vast breakdown within the Church and her ministry over the next two decades let alone constitute an adequate instrument for evangelical mobility. Declericalization may and should go far, but the Catholic Church cannot exist in authentic form without an adequately numerous and properly distributed priesthood—though not necessarily a very clerical one. While authority has accepted some declericalization of the ministry, it has largely lost its nerve when it comes to the priesthood: that, apparently, is to be left, a dwindling island of celibate sand as the tide flows in. Such a course would be disastrous. The renewal of the ministry already in hand must have at its core a major structural change in the sociological pattern of the priesthood itself. The appeal for such a change is not an appeal of despair nor an appeal for clerical permissiveness but an appeal in christian hope for a living ministry with a cutting edge, its own relevant asceticism and a capacity for survival in late twentieth-century society which the present structures simply do not have. It is also an appeal grounded in a careful appraisal of the Church's own history.

In setting forth upon a pilgrimage of ministerial discovery, there are elements of stability that the Church provides us with, elements that must be maintained and affirmed through any process of change. The first of these concerns what we can best call the primary ministry, that is to say the ministry of the whole

Church. No restructuring can alter the responsibility of the whole Church, the total people of God united in communion, in *koinonia*, to undertake the ministry of both *kerygma* and *diakonia*, of witness and of service. The reality of this primary responsibility should never be submerged by any sort of clericalism, frequently as this has in fact happened.

Secondly, this primary ministry is channelized and manifested through a great many different ministries responding to a variety of charisms and personal abilities, and only some of these ministries require the commissioning or ordaining of hierarchical authority. One has always to be on guard against the institutionalization of all the ministries of the Church. This is indeed a constant temptation to which the hierarchy is exposed: to admit other ministries only if they have been institutionalized and brought within the hierarchical system, made indeed into instruments of the hierarchy; we can see very clearly how this was happening in the age of Pius XI and Pius XII in regard to the great emergent movement of lay apostolate which was to be controlled as 'Catholic Action', an organization dependent upon the hierarchy's mandate. This was really to deny that there can be a non-hierarchical ministry within the Church.

The *kerygma*, the *diakonia*, the *koinonia* of the Church are the responsibility of all. And yet, thirdly, in a very important way the leadership in all these is also the special responsibility of a commissioned group. This ordained group, which represents apostolic authority within the different churches, is the backbone for the communion and mission of the whole Church; it has to articulate it, it has to trigger it off, strengthen it, lead it, but not dominate or swallow it up, not clericalize it, not even domesticate it. Its core function is to preside over the community gathered together for the celebration of the eucharist, just as the eucharist itself is the core of the Church. At the same time, this apostolically commissioned ministry both represents the local church to the wider church and represents the authority and the continuity of the wider church to the local church. This is what the priest of a parish does in relation to the wider community of the diocese: he represents both upwards and downwards. Equally the bishop, the chief minister of a diocese, both represents it in face of the Universal Church and represents the *Una Apostolica* to his own local church. Because he shares in the episcopal college, he can represent that college and the communion of all the other local churches which is signified by it to his own diocese, to his own *Ecclesia*.

Within and beyond these basic data of theology, is the overriding principle that the structuring of the ministry must be related to the contemporary pastoral needs of the Church, local and universal; not the other way round.

From this theological basis of what is inherent to the ministry of the Church (and it has here, of course, been very skimpily indicated), it is possible for many very different sociological patterns of ministry to grow. If anything is clear from history it is this, that the shape of the Church's ministry has varied enormously from age to age and place to place. A sociological comparison between the ministry of the apostolic Church, the ministry of the third and fourth centuries, the ministry of tenth-century Northern Europe, the ministry of seventeenth-century Southern Europe, the ministry of twentieth-century North America, would make this crystal clear. There has been a vast range of patterns as regards the kind of work chiefly done, the methods of selection and training, the degree of remuneration, the married or celibate status of the minister, the whole shape of the hierarchical structure and its mode of geographical extension. All these have altered radically time and again according to the pressures and needs of contemporary society and the contemporary Church. This does not mean that all the alterations of history have been desirable ones; very often, maybe, the Church has to a considerable extent succumbed in practice to undesirable pressures which have seriously weakened the effectiveness of its ministry, But equally desirable alterations may not have been made; conservative pressures within the Church may have canonized the pattern of a preceding age to such an extent that necessary reform has been delayed or prevented. The real point is that there is no one absolute pattern in itself wholly desirable but a series of patterns each of which to a greater or lesser extent has responded to the needs of a certain situation. Above all at a number of particular and crucial phases in the history of the Church, there has been a striking change in the pattern of ministry brought about by the inherent requirements of ministry within an enormously changed environment. These major and often relatively abrupt changes we can define as structural revolutions.

In approaching a consideration of the structural revolution needed today, it is very helpful to consider some earlier structural revolutions in Church history, and in particular that which occurred in the fourth and fifth centuries. It appears to me that what we need today is very comparable with the structural revolution of that time. What happened? There was, first, a vast population explosion within the Church. In the first three centuries the size of the Church, though steadily growing, remained relatively small. Individual local churches were kept down in their numbers by the pressure of the law, a hostile government, occasional persecution. But with the ending of those pressures and their replacement by imperial favour, the number of Christians grew enormously, multiplying in the towns and spilling over into the countryside to an extent that had not hitherto happened. Doubtless there were areas in the east where this process had already begun before the end of the third century, and there were areas in the west where it was a fifth-century phenomenon rather than a fourth-century one but the general process is clear. Certainly it had its disadvantages and the quality of normal Christian living may have deteriorated, but the Church could not refuse these people, yet equally it could not begin to cope with them through the old structures. As a consequence the whole shape and nature of a diocese as of the local ministry came to be changed.

Until that time the norm was to identify the eucharistic community with the diocese presided over by a bishop for which the classical picture has been provided by the letters of St Ignatius in the early second century. The presbyters were the bishop's advisers and substitutes on occasion but they were not typically the heads of independent congregations. Even towards the close of the fourth century this pattern of ministry could still be regarded as the norm and in the Milan of St Ambrose with its many tens of thousands of Christians, there might still be a single episcopal mass on a major feast day. Despite the grand new basilicas that were going up at the time, it was clearly now impossible for the majority of town Christians to attend mass on such a day. No basilica could house a church community of that size; only about one tenth of the Church of Milan could possibly have attended the episcopal mass. And a still more obvious problem than the multiplication of Christians within a town was that of all the Christian communities growing up in villages outside. The old pattern whereby the bishop was regarded as the normal minister of the Eucharist and the head of the local congregation (a pattern harked back to rather naively by the second Vatican Council) had now become deeply obstructive for the healthy life of the Church. Short of multiplying dioceses beyond all measure the idea of identifying the diocese with the eucharistic community had now become anachronistic. The consequence was the parish system. The diocese broke up into parishes and, instead of having one eucharistic community, the diocese came to consist of a great many congregations growing more and more independent. With the parishes emerges the order of the parochial clergy: the presbyter not the bishop had now become the basic pastor and normal president of the local eucharistic assembly; the bishop instead discovered his role as one of general pastoral oversight. A structural revolution had been forced upon the Church by the fact that the number of Christians, instead of being a matter of tens of thousands, had now become many millions. And only some sort of patristic fundamentalist will in principle regret it.

Roughly speaking it could be said that we have managed ever since with the structures that were created at that time. But that would really be an over-simplification for the Church's total ministry has been diversified and therefore greatly changed in its overall balance several times since then. This has happened particularly through the sudden structural revolutions which produced on a large scale congregations of men dedicated to specialized non-diocesan ministries. The first and really the most decisive of these revolutions took place in the early thirteenth century with the founding of the friars. There was, of course, great resistance to such a revolution on the part of contemporary ecclesiastical authority: the fourth Lateran Council (1215) actually forbade the establishment of any new religious order. But such resistance, as at many other moments of Church history, proved quite ineffectual. Despite the Lateran Council the Church's march to a more adapted and diversified ministry went on. It later proved indeed one of the great weaknesses of the post-Reformation Protestant churches that they dismantled the religious orders and returned to a too simplified and basically antiquated pattern of ministry, instead of purging and diversifying. Indeed when they were faced with the missionary challenge of the nineteenth century they were forced to establish new patterns of ministry, in the shape of the missionary societies, not wholly unlike the Catholic orders.

In the Catholic Church too the nineteenth century witnessed yet another major structural revolution, without which she could not possibly have responded effectively to the call of the times and the vast opportunities which were now appearing both in modern urban industrial society and overseas. On one side was the immense development of male missionary orders, many of them without vows, in the years after 1840; without them the newly opened up world would have remained almost entirely unevangelized from the Catholic side: their enormous expansion and characteristic life style has deeply altered the overall picture of the priestly ministry. On the other side, and still more remarkably, was the massive entry of women into the Church's active ministry, above all of teaching and nursing both at home and abroad. Up to the seventeenth century there was no consistent active participation of women in the Church's ministry at all, and in that century the attempt to bring it about was strongly resisted by ecclesiastical authority (Mary Ward, its great protagonist, was even imprisoned by the Pope) but it was not prevented. Yet it was only in the nineteenth century that it grew on a really large scale to alter the whole balance of the Church's organized ministerial effort. Today we take it for granted that the majority of the Church's active workers are women, restricted as their role still may be. This was a really formidable revolution and one only about a century old, without which the Church would have been quite incapable of responding to the opportunities of the modern world, and yet how many people advert to it today?

In each example of a structural revolution (from the very first one described in Acts 6) what happens is that, when faced with a new situation and large numbers of people, the ministry of the Church is diversified in new ways. That is true of the apostolic age; it is true of the fourth and fifth centuries; it is true of the development of religious orders and societies in the thirteenth, sixteenth and seventeenth centuries; it is true of the massive reorganization of the nineteenth century with its large-scale incorporation of women into the active ministry. It is true again of the structural revolution needed in our times when the Church is facing in the Third World a more massive population explosion than at any time since the fourth century.

To understand properly the shape that this revolution should take a good many things could be carefully analysed: the whole shape of a society and its income, the size and needs of local Christian communities, the position of women, the work of the priestly ministry as at present exercised in practice. Most of this it is impossible to do here. What one can quite easily see is how the type of priestly ministry that we have at present is seriously unrelated to the structure of the community: for example, the Catholic Church in Africa in reality consists for the most part of a vast number of fairly small village groups; the possible community can only be a small one of this kind, relating to the pressures of geography, the facts of daily life, the needs of non-motorized man. The small worshipping groups of the independent churches respond to the situation, as does the village chapel and the ministry of the catechist in the Catholic Church. But the present parochial and priestly ministry of the Church does not do so, dependent as it is upon the extremely small number of priests available so that each parish has to include dozens of villages and, often, dozens of churches; though it fulfils a worthwhile function of its own, operating in fact already as a supervisory and episcopal type of ministry but not as a form of community presbyterate. Yet the celebration of the eucharist is being tied canonically by the Church to this episcopal type of ministry instead of to the local presidency. And so, while at the level of theology more than ever before are we stressing that the eucharist is the necessary meaningful centre of the local Christian community, at the level of fact we are institutionally denying that truth more and more. Both eucharist and priesthood are today becoming of marginal significance in Christian life.

In many places the Church is in fact adjusting quite well to this extraordinary situation: it is going effectively congregationalist. The eucharist will be celebrated from time to time as a solemn extra when a priest from outside appears, but the life, worship and ministry of the real church is developing quite healthily on non-sacerdotal, non-presbyteral lines, led by catechists and other lay people. Something very similar is already beginning to happen in rural areas of France and Germany. Wise missionaries (and wise bishops in continental Europe) are fostering this movement, the only thing to do in circumstances where Catholic authority is effectively outlawing Catholic ministry. Of course such developments can in fact be the soundest basis for the new form of priesthood when it does come, for this should indeed develop out of the needs and existing structures of the local community and not be a further alien imposition.

To turn to an analysis of the present sociological shape of the priesthood, we can distinguish at least five issues which have to be objectively examined: these are, first, the question of full-time and part-time priests; secondly, finance; thirdly, the level of education and training required for priests; fourthly, the age of ordination; and fifthly, the matter of celibacy. Unless one is willing to face up to all these five questions, it is impossible to give a mature practical answer to the problem of reshaping the ministry.

As regards the issue of full-time or part-time priests, the first thing is to recognize that it is largely a matter of degree. It is presumed that hitherto nearly all priests have been 'full-time' and that the 'part-time' priests would be a great innovation; but in fact it is not so. Actually the life of priests is divided between a number of activities of different kinds. A great deal of time is spent in sleeping, eating, praying, writing letters, playing golf and so forth. Secondly, a very small amount of time is taken on what could be called explicitly priestly activities, that is activities which lay people are not allowed to undertake, such as presiding over the eucharist, hearing confessions, anointing the sick, but the number of hours that the vast majority of priests give to these activities is extremely limited. Thirdly, we have apostolic work of a general kind: pastoral visiting, counselling people in difficulty, visiting the sick, teaching religion in schools, and so forth. Now all these are quite properly the pastoral activities of the clergy but they are in no way exclusively so; they belong equally to the laity and indeed are primarily and properly lay activities; moreover they are of course, many of them, activities which sisters are engaged in full-time without having been ordained. Fourthly, there is a great deal of ecclesiastical administration which could just as well in principle be done by lay people; fifthly, and finally, a good many priests are engaged for a great part of their time in activities which are in no particular way connected with the priestly ministry, such as research, teaching mathematics in a secondary school, and so forth. We have always had a fair number of priests in such occupations.

Now there is no theological reason of any kind to dictate to what extent the activities of the ordained are going to be chiefly related to one of these fields rather than another, to what extent the general apostolate of the local church (such as counselling people in difficulty, visiting the sick) will be done by the clergy, by the laity, or by sisters; what proportion of priests are going to be involved for most of their time in 'secular' activities. We have always had a fair number of priests chiefly involved in secular work and if the consequence of a new pattern of ministry is that 60 or 70% of priests are engaged during the middle of the day from Monday to Friday in secular activities with only their week-end and evenings for pastoral or sacramental ministry while a minority of priests are engaged more or less full-time in activities more directly correlated to the Church's ministry, this is simply a matter of practical convenience. It has certainly happened before, and while it has its disadvantages, it has also its advantages.

The viability of one pattern or another depends in practice very considerably upon our second topic: finance. If priests are engaged most of the week in secular activities—as shop-keepers, government school teachers, or suchlike—they will not need to be supported by the Church. If, on the other hand, they are engaged most of the week in explicitly Church activities, then they have to be supported. A rich church can afford to support a large number of ministers full-time. Poor churches cannot afford to do so, especially if their ministers are fairly well educated. Now most churches in Africa are poor churches and are already facing a great shortage of finance, for they exist in countries where the average person's income a year may be no more than £30 or £40; not one tenth or even one twentieth of the average income in most countries of Europe and North America. It is natural therefore that in these churches one should seek for a particularly large number of ministers to be self-supporting, tent makers like St Paul. Clearly the question of finance relates not only to a full-time or part-time ministry but also in several ways to that of celibacy. In general, married priests need considerably higher salaries than unmarried. In our present system whereby very often two or three priests live together, quite clearly this is a way of providing rather cheap labour. It is perhaps worth noting that it is the rich churches like those of the United States and Holland, which are making most noise about ending the rule of celibacy: they won't have any great problem with regard to paying a married clergy. It is also understandable that on the whole African bishops, who are some of them facing near bankruptcy in their dioceses as it is, are mostly against ending the rule of celibacy—for they don't see how they would begin to provide for their clergy if the majority of priests were married. This is, clearly, a very practical and important question if one has as a major concern precisely the viability and self-reliance of the local church.

The correct conclusion, however, is not simply to perpetuate the present system which is breaking down anyway, but it does mean that if you are thinking in terms of married priests then you must also think of them in terms of being mostly self-supporting. One can see the same problem in the Anglican and Protestant churches, which have an almost entirely married clergy. In Africa their priests are mostly less educated than Catholic priests; even so they have considerable difficulty in providing them with a sufficient stipend. If their ministers were better educated, it is recognized that they would have to be paid still more. Again, to a large extent, the Catholic clergy in Africa today is supported on anonymous mass stipends coming from North America and Europe. This is in principle a deplorable system and it should be brought to an end because it is deplorable, theologically so. As a matter of hard fact, it is now on its way out. The supply is failing, and that again is creating immediate very practical material problems for our churches and can result in absolute penury for many good men. The present system of ministry will not in fact be financially viable in the future, and that is true not only for the Third World but for many churches in Europe too.

Thirdly, there is the question of the level and type of education a priest needs. Some people are absolutely against lowering the standard of education for any priest in any way. Many bishops have difficulty on this point. They fear the consequences of ordaining men who have not had a full secondary and then a full major seminary education. This is understandable particularly when it is reinforced by vague fears of various undesirable consequences and references to the state of the clergy in the middle ages, but it is mistaken. There is no correct level of education proper for a minister of the Church as such; of course there is a certain minimum, but the training and educational level of a priest needs to be related, far more than has been the case, to the community which he is working for and with. A village priest needs a very different kind of training from a university chaplain. As a matter of fact, if in some circumstances you can have a priest with too little education, in others you can have one who has too much; if you educate a man for a great many years and then put him in a deeply rural community where almost nobody else has any comparable education, he may very easily and quickly become frustrated: some will not do so but many will. Alternatively he may be completely paternalist. The education he received has not really related him to the type of ministry he has to exercise and the type of society he has to minister to. A far more flexible approach is needed here as in every other one of the fields we are considering.

Again, the educational pattern and professional training of the modern world is turning increasingly to in-service and up-dating courses. The old conception of education was that you started with a long apprenticeship, and would afterwards need no further training. You were set up for life. Priestly training continues to operate on this model and increasingly unsuccessfully. The shape of society and the problems to be tackled change so radically in one decade nowadays, that the only feasible way of training effective ministers is to provide far more up-dating and specialized courses for those already in the field. This means that the initial training ceases to have the final definitive character we still associate with the years in a seminary. In a modern training context these can be more easily cut down and indeed those who have had a lengthy old type seminary course can prove less responsive to later in-service training than others.

Fourthly, there is the age for ordination. Again we have taken for granted rather a rigid conception of this: twenty-four to thirty. Of course, of recent years there has been more talk of late vocations, but they are still considered as rather exceptional. I suspect that in the future ministry of the Church it may well be that a majority of priests will be ordained after the age of forty, and only a minority will be younger men. In fact it has often been quite a problem what to do with the immature young priest of twenty-four. No age is right in principle. Of course, if you are going to insist upon a long seminary training and celibacy for all priests, then indeed you have closed your options here too and you have to look predominantly for young men immediately upon leaving school or still at school. But all the signs of the times are against this. Once again the modern shape of society, shown in the increasing length of the average life span together with the relatively early age for retirement in many occupations, is creating the possibility of a quite new type of priestly recruitment on a large scale. The acceptable sociological shape for the ministry today will depend on such factors.

Fifthly, there is the issue of celibacy. No one, thinking seriously about it, is likely to argue that the mere changing of the law of clerical celibacy will solve the ministerial problems of the Catholic Church—the malaise and the need for readjustment go far deeper than that. Nevertheless, the nature of this law has been such as to force the whole pattern of ministry into certain directions, excluding a vast range of alternative options. Until the law is changed those options remain closed. Yet many of them are very sound ones. Their exclusion needs very strong theological reasons to justify it, particularly at a time when in practice a wholly celibate priestly ministry is clearly in the greatest difficulties. But these theological reasons simply do not exist. In scripture there is not the slightest indication that Christian ministers should not marry. On the contrary, St Paul takes it clearly for granted that most will be married men. How could that be the case if there was some strong intrinsic reason making for celibacy? The Vatican Council has firmly declared that the Church is subject to scripture, and we cannot apply in this field principles quite different from those which we accept elsewhere. Moreover Church history bears witness that if in the West there was for many centuries a tendency towards an ever greater insistence upon clerical celibacy, yet in every age the Church has also accepted married priests in one country or another and it already does so today. The positive content of the Catholic tradition includes a very strong assertion of the value of celibacy but it justifies no belittling of the value of marriage and has finally always refused to link the ministerial priesthood with one alone of these two states.

Today the theological defence of the present Western position generally takes the form of demonstrating the congruity of celibacy for a priest. True enough. But the congruity of a celibate priesthood does not in any way rule out an equal congruity in a married priesthood. Congruity means the harmonious relationship between two conditions. Such a relationship does exist between celibacy and the ministerial priesthood, but it equally exists between the latter and the sacrament of marriage. To deny this would be very perilous. But if something is highly congruous in theory, it should certainly not be wholly excluded in practice. In fact an argument from congruity is gravely misused when it is taken as proving that an alternative should be excluded. The Eastern practice whereby the priesthood is seen as essentially straddling these two states of life would seem to express the truly Catholic sense of the universality of the priesthood: it must not only offer the Mass and the ministry of the sacraments but a leadership within the Christian community which operates incarnationally from within, not externally—simply shouting instructions to the faithful from the safety of the touchline.

The universalization of clerical celibacy has in practice disparaged marriage. It has suggested that there is something about marriage so imperfect that it is not fitting for the ordained. The further effect of this has been that all the guidance the teaching church gives in this vast segment of life—sexual, marital and family responsibilities—has had to be done from outside, offered by people themselves never experiencing the implications of what they teach in their own life.

Moreover the rule has blurred celibacy's very sense. Its call, its charism, have not appeared with the clarity, the intrinsic meaning they do indeed possess: they appear in fact far more clearly in the world of women than in that of men, just because with women celibacy has been quite unrelated to priesthood. For men its sense will only re-emerge when the vocational difference between the religious life and that of the pastoral clergy is again made precise.

Again, it is absurd to disregard the sound, and at times saintly, experience of a married priestly ministry in the Orthodox, Anglican and Protestant churches: nothing is more depressing than the almost contemptuous way in which Catholics have often spoken of the married priesthood outside their own communion

—and even within their communion, in the Eastern uniate rites. It enables the priesthood to be linked with, for example, the virtue of hospitality (one of the most characteristic biblical and Christian virtues), a thing which has almost disappeared, being labelled dangerous, within the celibate clerical world.

Celibacy is an important and fruitful calling in its own right place and its recognition (so derided at the Reformation) has been an immense source of strength to the Catholic Church in comparison with the Reformed Churches, particularly within the missionary ministry; but it is essentially—when it passes beyond the limits of a private decision—part of the calling to a religious order, be it 'active' or 'contemplative'. Much of the strength of the Catholic ministerial tradition has lain in the major divide between its 'secular' and its 'religious' sectors, but this divide has been steadily and unhappily eroded over the last centuries. Its renewed recognition can be nothing but a benefit—and to both sides. While the present debate over celibacy is essentially a matter for the seculars, it is in practice wrecking havoc with the religious orders, and it is probable that the crisis within the latter cannot be even partially resolved and their own identity reaffirmed before the Church positively recognizes the regularity and desirability of a non-religious, non-celibate pastoral clergy.

We are being called in this age to a new appraisal of the structures of the Church in the light of the Gospel and the shape of human society. To right the inevitable imbalances of the past. It would be absurd and a new imbalance to decry the value of celibacy or its capacity for fruitfulness in human living and many patterns of ministry; but we must not be anti-marriage either and it would be hard indeed to show the Western canonical tradition of celibacy has not owed much to a profound theological and spiritual depreciation of marriage. Only from a balanced vision, which gives its due to both, can we go forward as we must to a ministry which welcomes not only the celibate but the married, and not only the ordination of the married but the marriage of the ordained.

The future shape of the Church's ministry will vary from continent to continent, country to country, city to isolated rural community, just as it has in practice always done but probably (at least for a time) the divergencies will grow rather than diminish as we understand better the implications of coping both with New York and with Norway, both with Northern Nigeria and with Nicaragua, both with the Netherlands and North Vietnam. In Africa too there will be far from only one pattern. The shape of society enormously varies between the big towns and the deep rural areas; some rather thickly populated countryside and much that is extremely thin; areas with a cash crop and an expanding economy and areas of extreme poverty and subsistence farming; areas in which Christians are numerous, others in which they are very few. These differences are certainly not going to disappear in the next twenty-five years and the Church's ministry must be structured accordingly.

Nevertheless, nearly everywhere there are likely to be four chief elements in the ministry requiring to be related to one another in a variety of ways. The first element we will speak of is the new kind of priest. Many in this group will be active professional and business people who will operate as part-time priests and be supported by their work; some will be retired men living on a pension: some will be chosen from among the thousands of catechists working in Africa and Asia today. As ordained catechists they will be supported by the Church to roughly the same extent as they are at present as unordained catechists. Most dioceses in Africa have some hundreds of catechists; their training standards and amount of work greatly vary, but they have in many places been given much help over the last ten years with the greater stress on catechist formation that has now become prevalent, and it does not appear wildly ambitious to suggest that over a period of five years 10% of them could, with further training, be ordained. This could make a staggering difference to the pastoral and missionary effectiveness of the Church of 1980. It would bring the eucharist back into the heart of the local church, where it should so essentially be but now increasingly cannot be. It may well be that the new kind of priest will often work as one of a team of such men rather than as the sole ordained minister in a place, but either model can be appropriate.

This does not, of course, mean that every congregation or village church in Africa, France or England must have its own priest or priests; as things are at present that is hardly possible, and probably not necessary. The basic aim should be that at least every group of some four or five village churches have a priest between them, who is a man living within their community, not outside it, and that every congregation be able to celebrate the eucharist at least once a month.

The qualifications to be insisted upon in all cases are: first, holiness, a real dedication to the work of God, to the service of the Church and of other men; secondly, human maturity and balance of character; and thirdly, a sufficient minimum of theological education so that they can properly understand their duties and participate intelligently in the initial training and subsequent refresher courses.

Among the new priests there will not be only one classification. Some will certainly be very much part-time, but others could be full-time. Some of the new men may be even better educated than the present priests, and after ordination may make greater efforts to keep up with theological developments. It has at least been found to be so in other Churches: some tent-making ministers subsequently read more theology than those who have had a standard seminary training. It would be a mistake to plan one fixed form of initial training for new kinds of priests: for catechists it should be possible to arrange a full year, or more, in one of the present catechist centres or some comparable place. But for many professional and business people, ordination training will have to be done chiefly by correspondence stiffened by a series of rather short residential courses. Clearly all will need to reach a certain standard of knowledge, of a relevant pastoral sort. Over the years these various groups will probably come together to form a considerable majority, and this means that a large proportion of priests are likely to be married.

In the present situation in the Church the ordination to the diaconate is a suitable half-way house in the restructuring of the ministry and it may, indeed, be of real value to have a half-way house of this kind. As we are now allowed to train men and to ordain them to the diaconate, to ordain married men thus far is what we ought to be doing now and it is a great pity and a sign of shortsightedness that the Churches in Africa are not doing so on a larger scale while the Churches of Europe and North America are. It is, of course, very possible that the recent revival of the diaconate as a mini-priesthood (that is to say doing all the present duties of a priest, short of saying mass and hearing confession) is basically a conservative attempt to avoid what is really needed, the priestly ordination of married men, by misusing a different ministry. The diaconate's real function should rather be institutionalized service; *diakonia* in the sense of secular concern. This may well be true. At the same time the original meaning of the diaconate as a particularized ministry and also its historical development, are far from clear. Probably we have misused the diaconate for many hundreds of years by making it simply a final stepping-stone in the curriculum of the seminary. If it has already been misused in a non-pastoral way and if today we to some extent misuse it again (but this time for good pastoral purposes) then let us for a while do so. The point is that we are allowed to do this now, and by doing it we can select men, train them, and give them extra immediate responsibilities so that when the Universal Church comes to agree that married men should be ordained as priests, then the candidates are there and ready.

There will certainly remain the greatest need for a smaller group of very professional priests with a still more intensive theological training than is today offered. These will nearly all be more or less full-time ministers. Some will be members of religious orders, others diocesan; all the former will be celibate and some of the latter. It is essential that there be men in every local church with a full theological education and, while a theologian does not need to be ordained, it is to be expected that among our theologians many will be priests. In a way, they will be involved in the sort of ministry that in the past has been associated with the episcopate, that is to say oversight: *episcope*. They will not, because they will be far too few, be the normal ministers of word and eucharist in individual Christian communities, at least in South America and Africa. African rural parishes already often consist of twenty or more communities which ought each to have a regular celebration of word and eucharist but cannot receive it; in many dioceses today there are no more than four, five or six local priests and very few seminarians. Such dioceses have mostly some twenty parishes and over three hundred major worshipping centres. It is clear as day that such a small group cannot possibly provide the regular pastoral ministry. What they will have to do is to serve the local priests who are going to provide the pastoral ministry. The function of the fully trained clergy will be to run some of the central parishes and the training colleges and to provide updating courses for both clergy and laity. They will frequently be travelling missioners, providing, in fact, a pre-eminently kerygmatic ministry, in striking contrast with the rather limited concern for the word and major preoccupation with the sacraments forced upon the fully-trained clergy at present. It is greatly to be hoped that among these priests there will be a considerable number of members of religious orders. The Catholic Church's ministry in the past has been immensely strengthened and enriched by the diversity of the religious orders and the need for them will be no less great in the future, precisely because they can provide far more explicitly than can the diocesan clergy a 'Catholic', inter-diocesan, international type of ministry.

Evidently these different groups will need to work together. Just as it would be disastrous to continue with only a small group of seminary-trained men, so it could be disastrous to have only a clergy with rather limited training, without any priests with a lengthier theological education. One group will not be better than the other; each will have its own strength. Just as members of religious orders are not better than seculars, just different. Each group has to balance an other and without the more highly trained and professional, more full-time, probably more celibate groups, the others could lead in the direction of a rather inturned Church. It is a criticism of the Eastern Churches that with an almost entirely married clergy, of somewhat limited education, they have become very inward looking, without much sense of mission. This is surely an oversimplification of a complex phenomenon; nevertheless it has some truth in it. It will be especially for the 'full-time' priests, some of whom will certainly continue to be celibate, to contribute particularly to the wider sense of both mission and communion and to ensure the doctrinal and theological standards of the local church (functions in the Eastern Churches fulfilled particularly by monks). We have simply to recognize that both groups have an essential role to play within the ministry of the Church of the future.

A third and most important group is that of the sisters. We have spoken already of that vast structural revolution in the nineteenth-century Church whereby women entered on a large scale into the active organized ministry of the Church both at home and in missionary situations. In this way religious sisters undoubtedly took a front place in the 'women's liberation' of that age as well as enabling the Church as a whole to respond to the educational and medical needs of the time to an extent which would otherwise have been quite impossible. What is needed today is a further leap forward in the same direction. Up till now the ministerial role of sisters has remained mostly within the environment of school and hospital. Today, without abandoning this kind of work, they need to enter extensively into many other social and pastoral fields of activity: social work, catechetical work, counselling, the intensive visiting of an area, the provision of special courses of instruction, and—in some places—the regular running of a parish. There are undoubtedly sides of the Church's organized work which women can do far better than men and the Church's healthy development in this age of an ever increasing women's liberation requires that many women, both lay and religious, enter into them.

Women, lay and religious, are called today to every side of the ministry, to *kerygma* and *diakonia*, to building up the full *koinonia* of the Church. It is a shame both for them and for the Christian community that they should still largely be confined or feel themselves confined to one or two traditional forms of institutionalized work.

In Brazil, in Uganda and elsewhere there are in fact parishes run by sisters on their own. The sheer scarcity of priests has forced the bishops to it, but they do it very well. They baptize, lead the worship of the congregation, give out holy communion, preach, visit homes, encourage and assist community development.

In the context of today we can no longer close our eyes to the possibility of women priests. No convincing argument has been found against the ordination of a woman. In the past the question hardly arose because of a whole pattern of society and the position of women in it, but today it does—not only because of general changes in the world but also because of changes which have already taken place or are now rapidly taking place within the Church. What is of particular importance to cling to in the ordering of the Christian ministry is the close relationship of word and sacrament and the congruity that someone who is the regular community minister of the one should also be minister of the other. Those who regularly preach and even give communion should also be ordained to celebrate and preside at mass. Having decided in principle that women can and should do the one, it will be difficult for very long to deny them the other without creating a new artificial imbalance within the ministry. Doubtless this will not be agreed upon without much discussion, prayer and struggle, and we have enough to struggle about as it is, but the evolution of the ministry and the position of women within it will make it increasingly necessary to face up to this in coming years.

Fourthly, and most important of all, we come back to the ministry of the lay community. All other ministries must finally be seen as ways to stimulate and articulate the work of the community as a whole, and it is remarkable how alive and responsible a small community can become when it is really treated as an adult missionary fellowship to be directed by its own parish council working with its priest. The parish council is to be seen as having in consultation with him, the decisive responsibility not only for the collecting of money and its spending but for the basic liturgical, pastoral and missionary planning of the local church. There are places where this is indeed developing very effectively. In Africa is is generally not the parish council—on present terms—but the priestless sub-parish council which is becoming the decisive body. It is here that the local congregation can gather to plan its ministry, and the parish council is to be seen as a federation of sub-parish councils, and the diocesan pastoral council in its turn as a federation of parish councils. The corporate life of the local lay community implies a continuous diversification of ministries whereby some members of the congregation have particular liturgical and preaching responsibilities, others are assigned for teaching catechism at school, others again for leadership in the area of social development, still others for visiting the sick, laying hands upon them and praying with them. All these can be members of the lay community and will, of course, include women as well as men.

These are the ministries of the local community; they will be co-operating with a priest, not so far removed from them, who will have nevertheless responsibility for several other congregations as well. He is likely to be a married man and probably not young. Both he and his congregations will be immensely helped by the full-time and far more highly qualified priest who will from time to time come to visit, to instruct, and to keep the church in touch with the rest of the diocese; they will also be helped by sisters. They may be so lucky as to have a house of sisters in their area but more probably they will simply receive a visit from an occasional peripatetic team to provide extra instruction and stimulation. Both local priests and lay readers will also, of course, go away from time to time for retreats, refresher courses, and the experience of a wider ministerial fellowship.

A ministry of this type including both men and women, both priests and lay men, both the full-time and the part-time, both the married and the celibate, both the local diocesan clergy and the inter-diocesan, international religious order, will have an immense strength of its own. The priesthood will then manifestly cease to be what it has at times seemed to be—an area of uniformity and of internal oppression. While at present there is a feeling, both within and without clergy ranks, that the young priest has often been almost conned into signing away his basic right to marry, the acceptance of a diversified ministry will enable the priest, whether celibate or married, to appear to the world what he should be par excellence—a free man. All this is not a day dream but a feasible reality if the Church has the will to bring it about, and in that case the present age, far from witnessing a painful and destructive collapse of the Church's ministry, will be one instead of a magnificent renewal, enrichment and fruitfulness. We will then have indeed a strong, healthy, diversified ministry to offer the Church of the future, a future for which there need be no fear.

12

Death transformed

Each year as one approaches Holy Week and Good Friday a Christian is forcibly reminded that Sister Death is at the very centre of his religion. Whatever else it does, the crucifix proclaims significance in a death. As such death is simply a physical fact and a human experience, part of the givenness of the world, but here as everywhere Christian faith takes the facts and experiences of the world and interprets them according to their meaning and ethical possibilities. It both uncovers an existent meaning and injects more in the light of Christ and the life of the Spirit. Death presents a host of intellectual and moral problems, more for our generation perhaps than ever before; to face them we have to return to the central Christian affirmations as we discover them in Jesus himself.

The decisive characteristic of Jesus's own death was its voluntary character. Jesus chose to die. All four evangelists hammer home this point time and again and the theology of redemption hinges upon it. Our celebration of the Eucharist can indeed exist as the continuing sacrament of his creative death, because and only because when he was a free man only a few hours earlier he chose to make it so. By freely choosing to die, by deliberately going up to Jerusalem and staying there at a time when with absolute certainty he could see that this would bring about his killing, he was able to transform death not only for himself but for us. It is not the pain but the freedom that is the final point of the crucifix, providing us with the way all men need to face death, transforming it into victory. Freedom transfigures death: that is the lesson we have to learn again and again. The Christian attitude to death is certainly not to rush into it with bravado, Christ never did that; but equally it is not to put it off, to avoid it, at all costs. It is to claim with confidence that death can be faced, mastered and transfigured.

The first affirmed theme of sanctity was found just here—the martyrs are people who voluntarily chose to die for God or for others and who, by doing so, each time removed death's sting. It is indeed a position of faith, but it is also a position that has been verified experientially time and again. Take one of the few people of our own time whose outstanding holiness has already been confirmed by the authority of the Church: the Polish priest Maximilian Kolbe. In 1941 in Auschwitz concentration camp he freely offered to die, to replace a fellow prisoner in the starvation shed where ten men were to be confined as punishment for the escape of a prisoner from the camp. His voluntary presence transformed that shed; in place of the howling and cursing that had so often been heard in similar situations, he led his companions in praying and singing through the long days of dying. In freedom he transfigured his own death and that of others too.

Difficult as it is in the life of each of us to come in depth to share such an attitude, it is of the essence of Christian commitment that we struggle towards it; it is part of the core of hope—one's view of the future—and is integral to the pastoral care of others and to participation in the public debate on euthanasia and other issues. An approach to the latter will be shallow and inauthentic if it simply overlooks the basic truth that the Christian position starts from the belief that the new Adam chose to die for his brother men.

In choosing to die the first thing is that we must be allowed to know that we are dying. A letter from a priest recently informed me that an old friend, an elderly priest, was dying from cancer. I was urged not to mention this. He himself had not been informed. 'Please respect this taboo.' Our friend died only a few weeks later. I am glad at least that the letter writer did not suggest that what he was requesting was a Christian line of action. He subconsciously fell back upon a pre-Christian word to express a post-Christian line of action, which meant depriving our friend of the chance for adequate time in which to die responsibly and freely. Recently I was reading the *Memoirs* of Manya Harari, that very remarkable Russian Jewish convert to Christianity and Catholicism. When in 1969 she learnt that she was dying she wrote: 'Being ill and dying is a job, in a sense like any other, but of course an important one. The important thing is to do it as well as one can. I find the knowing about it in advance, however uncertain the date, but with a knowledge more precise than one has when one is well is something so real, factual and also demanding, that it leaves one hardly any room for nostalgia or sadness for oneself, or even for regretting what one hasn't managed to get done in life.'

Likewise Boswell tells us how when Samuel Johnson, a man who had greatly feared to die, was near to it he 'asked Dr Brocklesby, as a man in whom he had confidence, to tell him plainly whether he could recover. "Give me (said he) a direct answer." The Doctor having first asked him if he could bear the whole truth, which way soever it might lead, and being answered that he could, declared that, in his opinion, he could not recover without a miracle. "Then (said Johnson), I will take no more physic, not even my opiates; for I have prayed that I may render up my soul to God unclouded." In this resolution he persevered.'

Dr Johnson and Mrs Harari were very strong-minded people, but there is no reason whatever to think that others cannot do the same, that the Holy Spirit will not strengthen them if they are but given the chance, being treated in an essentially human and Christian manner. The words we have cited suggest a true approach towards the spirituality of dying and the ministry to the dying—a ministry that underestimates neither their rights, nor their capacity, nor the seriousness of the moment, nor—above all—the meaningfulness of Christ's conquest of death.

There are very great dangers in any form of legalised euthanasia, particularly perhaps in the opportunity it could give for relations or medical staff to put pressure on an old sick person to sign life away. It is the task of the Church as of the law to guard above all the rights of the weak. And there are immense practical problems in deciding when one should cease to try hard to prolong the life of another, senile or semi-senile. If it is ridiculous to imagine that charity will always struggle to prolong another's life and if there are extreme cases over which almost anyone would agree, there are many others where a decision must be intensely difficult. Practical judgements so often are. Modern medicine has made it impossible and irresponsible simply to shrug off these problems; it is now becoming too easy to keep a vegetable alive almost indefinitely if money is available. And it is not clear at all that the mere prolongation of an absolutely restricted life is in itself of value or of moral obligation. Yet in practice almost any generalisation seems to lead one on to very dubious and dangerous ground.

Certainly one important distinction to cling to is the difference between imposing death upon another and choosing it for oneself. It is strange how hard Christians have often judged suicide, how easily they have justified capital punishment even for quite trivial offences, for the thrust of our faith is quite the other way. We must not take the lives of others, but we can offer up our own. Captain Oates does not need any devious moral justification; he did a deeply and obviously Christian thing. A person coming near to death should not be told that it is gravely immoral to end one's life for a weighty reason, to avoid being a heavy burden to others—for example—or so as to die when one can still render up one's soul unclouded and not after months of a merely vegetable existence. The choice of death can seem justified for many reasons that make it an act of faith and love, not of despair or the rejection of God. But what is centrally important is to see the responsible acceptance of death as the finally most mature decision of our human existence and to prepare to face death oneself, and help others face death, unlied to and, so far as possible, undrugged.

Biologically death is the antithesis of life, but theologically it is not and cannot be so. Death has been mastered by the Lord of Life, and if we do not believe that, we have no Christian faith. The psychological agony of dying is no less—the dissolution of one's body cannot but be a fearful experience. And yet, despite that, a 'happy death' is not an impossibility as facts fully demonstrate: the interpretation of faith proves existentially stronger than the interpretation of nature. The true sanctity of life is not endangered by dying, and the starting point for Christian thinking about one's own dying and the support of others who are dying is not some abstract sanctity of life, but the holy freedom of death, a liberation which, grounded in Christ's death, shares in the fullness of that Christian freedom which takes all things seriously but is enslaved by none.

13

Christus resurrexit, alleluia

'If Christ has not been raised, then our preaching is useless and your believing is useless' (I Cor. 15:14). So Paul affirmed as unambiguously as he could, in his first letter to the Corinthians some twenty-five years after the end of Jesus' life on earth. In it he emphatically declares that the statement 'Christ has been raised to life' was the key teaching he had already given them some eight years earlier and that it was what he himself had been taught a good many years before that.

There can be no possible doubt that according to our earliest evidence Christ's resurrection was the very core of the Christian message, and his resurrection was clearly understood by our chief preacher and witness, Paul, in a factual, not a mythical, way. But it was hard to believe, and already Paul is having to reply to doubters at Corinth who can accept the moral and spiritual dimensions of his message but not the absurdity of this hard historic claim. 'Christ rose on the third day.' Today as much as then the knife edge of Christian faith is here; indeed, enquiry into the authentic meaning of the resurrection is coming to take very clearly the central place in the contemporary battle over the integrity and significant survival of christianity as faith. It is striking how many books and articles have appeared recently on this theme. It seems as if the whole intense re-examination of Christian life and belief which has been gathering momentum for years has now reached this root point of origin, and this not just for a few academics but for very large numbers of people caught up in the catechetical movement and in other areas of theological thought.

What do we mean by the resurrection of Jesus? Was it a historical event or a symbol-laden myth? Does it matter much one way or the other? The difficulties with the former view are undoubtedly great. First come the obvious and numerous inconsistencies between the Gospel narratives: was Jerusalem or Galilee the location of the meetings with the disciples? One angel or two? One woman or more? and so much else. Furthermore, a careful reading of the texts shows only too clearly how the earliest references add little detail to the sheer proclamation of the fact of the risen Christ while the later accounts provide long and detailed stories of an almost earthly if still mysterious Jesus sitting round, eating, carrying on long conversations. As the years went by, one asks, did not the imagination of the believers get the better of them into weaving more and more symbolic but non-factual stories? And if we once admit the possibility of that, can we be sure that any of the stories, even the earliest, are historically reliable, and not just the fruit of the inspired imaginings of the early Christians? Then come the philosophical and scientific doubts: is it really conceivable that a corpse was resuscitated? And, if so, what happened to it afterwards? Could it really be whisked away to a non-spatial 'heaven'? Is it not all just a glorious myth whose truth content is quite detachable from any historicity in the events? Are the bones of Jesus not really there in the soil of Palestine?

It is of course Rudolf Bultmann, most influential of the scripture scholars of this century, who would have it so: the resurrection is the believing way of understanding Calvary. The Jesus who died on Calvary has been glorified by God. But the resurrection has no true status as 'event' between the death on the cross and the subsequent conviction of the disciples that their master was alive with God and indeed most favoured of God. To explain this conviction they produced stories about their meetings with the living Christ. Other theologians would explain the resurrection myth, not so much as an interpretation of Jesus' death alone, but as a reflection upon his whole life in the light of the Old Testament and under the inspiration of the Spirit. The stories about apparitions and the empty tomb were either without historical foundation or were at best psychological experiences consequent upon an already existing belief. Many Christians, including Catholics, are now arguing that such is the case, and they do so in all believing sincerity. They do not feel that this weakens the true meaning of the Resurrection: Jesus Christ truly triumphed over death and he promises in faith that we may do the same.

I accept the sincerity of such views, but I do not the less profoundly disagree with their conclusions, which would seem to me objectively destructive of the whole system of Christian belief and, with it, Christian revolutionary dynamism. It is a grave erosion of the Easter faith.

From a purely scholarly point of view one can certainly not

come to an agreed conclusion. The arguments put forth against belief in a historical resurrection are plausible but essentially not compelling. No one considers evidence here or elsewhere without philosophical presuppositions, without his own subtle sense of the limits of the possible and the credible. The very fact that Christian faith asserts and has always asserted the resurrection of Jesus to be unique means that it is intrinsically exempt from scientific objection. Science can only say: we know no other example of this and can therefore not comment about how it happened or could happen—but that is exactly what Christian doctrine has itself always said. We do not know the mind of God except in so far as he has revealed it to us, so we cannot argue *a priori* whether at this central point of human history he would or would not will things to happen which are never experienced at other times. But if we say on principle that he would not, or did not, we must either be claiming to know his mind in some other way or be saying that we do not consider this was after all so absolutely and uniquely the centre of human history. And this latter, I suspect, is what the anti-historicists are in fact saying. Despite much deep personal devotion they are objectively reducing the significance of Jesus Christ and even removing any credible ground for asserting his religious uniqueness in any absolute way.

One of the great practical weaknesses in any theory that the disciples simply came to believe in the resurrection as a result of meditating upon the life and death of Jesus in the light of the Old Testament, is that the Old Testament really does not offer any great help in the matter. There is nothing there sufficient to make them believe that in some uniquely extraordinary way Jesus must rise in triumphant life soon after his death, unless they had in fact experienced it, as the Gospels claimed they did, through a series of apparitions following upon the discovery of the empty tomb. Remove all historicity from those accounts and you make a historical nonsense of a far wider story. Both faith and reason concur in the conclusion that soon after Christ's burial something happened within historical experience that manifested Christ to be the risen Lord, the 'first fruits' of the resurrection of the dead which is still to come. The general resurrection is the end of history, it is our final future and beyond time, even if it be experienced in some way immediately after death by those who die in Christ. Such experience is essentially non-historical. But what we affirm at Easter is that in Jesus the end has already happened, and has happened somehow within history. Only a 'first fruits' within history can justify in Christian terms hope in a final resurrection beyond history. It is of the essence of Christian belief that it flows out from the particular, the historical and the physical; if that is true, it must be true above all of the source of all our belief, the Resurrection, key point of the kerygma.

The details of the appearances are not important; if there were many appearances (and some of the very earliest evidence, in I Corinthians, says that there were), and if as is understandable people were for long reluctant to write in detail of such fundamental, emotional, intimate, and unparalleled experiences, and if their full meaning only emerged over the years (and that is true of many intense human experiences) then it is not surprising that there is some confusion and even embroidery in the final accounts. What they all affirm is that, having died and been buried, Jesus rose on the third day and was seen by many. What his risen body was like or where it went, we have no idea, but—accepting the corporeal nature of man—we must affirm the continuity of his risen body with his dead body, and this continuity is not compatible with the idea that his dead body remained untouched in the grave.

Christ's resurrection was not a historical event in the obvious sense: it was not itself reported or observed; again, it was intrinsically not historical in a deeper sense because it precisely signifies his passage into a state beyond history. Yet it is historical in several important ways: first, it had immediate historical consequences—the empty tomb, the manifestations to his disciples, which were part of their temporal history; secondly, and still more profoundly, because in its meaning it is part of history—it is not merely the manifestation of non-temporal truth, but the establishment of the ultimate already now within the temporal and particular order, so that it could be given a historic tense. The claim to such an establishment is, of course, the supreme scandal to the unbeliever and to many spiritually minded theologians as well. From the beginning the Church preached the resurrection not in the present but in the past tense: 'Jesus has risen' not 'Jesus is alive'. The tense is vital, it implies historicity and is not to be whittled away.

These are not fine academic points. All the drive and the joy in our life will follow from them. True Christian moral commitment is a passionate concern with the particular and the material. Its grounding is in the particularity, the historicity, the materiality of Incarnation, Resurrection and Eucharist. The spiritualists and the demythologisers, for all their sincerity and all their devotion, hold to a different Christ and a different

Gospel. Their spiritual resurrections and communions have no power to overturn the world of flesh, the segregation of race, the torture of the body. It is the risen flesh of the Incarnate Lord sacramentally present in the Eucharist which transforms a spiritual philosophy into a revolutionary creed. God willed it so and we must not yield the precious pearl of historicity and materiality to any demythologisers, learned and devout as they may be.

Christ has risen, alleluia.

125